T0353763

NEW WINE SKINS

Living Jesus's Teachings in the Age of Science

ALLEN A. SWEET

Skins

LIVING JESUS'S TEACHINGS IN THE AGE OF SCIENCE

iUniverse books may be ordered through booksellers or by contacting:

iUniverse
1663 Liberty Drive
Bloomington, IN 47403
www.iuniverse.com
1-800-Authors (1-800-288-4677)

ISBN: 978-1-6632-0473-8 (sc)
ISBN: 978-1-6632-0474-5 (e)

Library of Congress Control Number: 2020912235

Print information available on the last page.

iUniverse rev. date: 07/16/2020

Contents

Preface

As I write the preface to this book, my wife, Fran, and I are locked in our apartment in self-imposed isolation as a measure of safety in the face of the dangers caused by the coronavirus pandemic that is sweeping our world in 2020 CE. Nobody comes to visit us, and we go nowhere. Our children regularly bring us food and other supplies. Fran is an Alzheimer's victim. It is terribly sad, and I feel so helpless. Her doctor has tried numerous medications, but nothing seems to help. All I can really do for her is give her my sympathy, compassion, and kindness. There really isn't much else I can do except for all the practical stuff that must be done anyway.

My earliest memories of Jesus go back to my Sunday school days as a small child. Mom and Dad took me to Sunday school each week, and I came to enjoy the Bible stories as I learned about Noah, his ark, and his animals (How did Mrs. Noah stand it?). I also fondly remember the Passover story when God fought for his people to rescue them from slavery. What a wonderful story in any age.

When Sunday school was over, I would join my parents in "Big Church" to hear sermons that were usually over my head, using words like *sin* and *forgiveness*. I already knew about forgiveness after having some of my misbehaviors discovered by Mom or Dad, but I had no idea what sin was. However, what I really looked forward to most in Big Church were the stories about Jesus and his teachings. Right away, I was taken by how easily some of Jesus's words fit right into my life and how the people of Jesus's time were so attentive to his every word.

At some point, Jesus became my own personal hero. I wanted to be like him in every possible way. I was particularly attracted to Jesus's advice that if someone does something wrong to you, don't fight with them. Instead, offer to let them do the wrong again (turn the other cheek).

I am an only child—and so is Fran—so I had no experience with roughhousing and fighting with brothers and sisters. When I began to have trouble with schoolyard bullies, Jesus's words took on real meaning in my life. When being tormented by one of these bullies, I would just stand there and take it. I wouldn't tell them to stop or run; I would just stand there. Pretty soon, more bullies started enjoying the sport of bullying me. My parents found out about the bullying and wondered why I didn't defend myself. I didn't know how to tell them I was just following advice I had learned in church. At that point, I began to realize why Jesus had taught his followers that the world will not understand you—and even your own family may not understand you.

The worst time of year for me was Holy Week. It contained the Friday when my hero was murdered in the most horrible way imaginable. Every Good Friday—I never understood why it is called *good*—I would get up very early and spend the entire day in the woods. My mom tried to convince me to go to a free movie that was shown for the local children each Good Friday, depicting the events of Holy Week and Good Friday. Why would I want to go to a movie—free or otherwise—in which my hero is murdered in the most horrible way imaginable? I always came up with some excuse for why I couldn't go until she finally stopped asking.

My day in the woods saw me sitting by a river. I was watching the ducks and the muskrats swimming upstream and downstream. As I sat, I thought about my dying hero and what he must have gone through. It made me so sad that tears started falling like rain as I watched the ducks paddle back and forth. However, there was one part of the Good Friday story that gave me comfort when I realized during a Gospel reading in church that Jesus had to confront bullies in his day in the form of powerful political and religious leaders. These so-called leaders asked Jesus horrible questions about his relationship with God. They taunted Jesus in the same way that I was being taunted by the schoolyard bullies. This made me realize that Jesus followed his own advice and that I, when confronted by the schoolyard bullies, had acted as my hero wished me to act. At least I gained the satisfaction that I was traveling on the right path with the right hero.

Aside from the bullies in the schoolyard, my life inside the classroom was slowly going from bad to worse. I was having problems with reading and spelling. In truth, I couldn't read at all. It is very hard to do anything else in the early grades if you can't read, and I couldn't! My teachers blamed me. My report cards held notices like "Does not apply himself," "Daydreams," "Wastes time," and "Does not work up to his potential." These reports were starting to cause big problems at home.

Mom took on my reading problem as a personal crusade. She got special books to help me make progress with reading. Instead of making progress in reading, we were making progress in anger and tears for us both. Looking back, I think I suffered from some degree of dyslexia. However, in the early fifties, this was still an unknown concept.

The crisis came when our school's administration sent a special test teacher to spend three days with me to determine what my real problem was. At first, she seemed nice. She told me up front that all of the tests were to be given orally since I couldn't read. She asked me endless questions, and I gave her the best answers I knew how to give.

At the end of three days, she told me that all of the testing had been completed, and she would share the results with me. She said that I was in no way intellectually disabled; on the contrary, I was very bright. However, in her opinion, I was lazy and unmotivated and seemed unable to keep focus on working hard to improve my reading. She shared with me that the only reason I had advanced to a higher grade each year, for a number of years now, was to keep me from looking "too big" for my grade. In truth, I had totally failed every attempt to teach me anything for the past several years.

Her final threat was that during the next year, I would be starting junior high school with rotating class, each conducting a different subject in a different room, rather than spending the entire day in the same classroom. However, if I failed to make "reasonable" grades in my first year in junior high school, I would be transferred into a special education program. I was devastated and terrified. I already knew what special education looked like, and I knew I didn't belong there. I am sure Mom and Dad were told the results of the testing, but they never said a word about it to me. Perhaps they had decided it was all up to me to get myself out of this mess.

Two years prior, my dad had given me a little crystal radio kit for Christmas. He fondly remembered his own crystal radio from childhood and hoped I would have a similar enjoyable experience. I loved the crystal radio! I was fascinated with it in so many ways. I had never been so fascinated before. Everything about it was earthshakingly wonderful to me. The little "cat's whisker" begged me to adjust it to bring in a more distant station with its tiny "whisker" adjustment.

At night, I often heard "skip" stations coming in from places like Detroit or Saint Louis. I was in love, and I had a million ideas about how I could improve my little crystal set. However, to make these radio improvements, I would first have to read about what others had done to improve similar radios.

To improve my little crystal radio, my first challenge was learning to read. Believe it or not, I did just that before the summer was over. I went into that summer as a nonreader with a little crystal set I loved, and I came out of the summer with a much more complicated crystal set and the new ability to read! I was off to junior high school to be a success and to stay out of special education forever. My prayers had been answered; my hero, Jesus, had not let me down!

As it turned out, I was more than saved from the threat of special education. In fact, my life changed drastically for the better. In the words of my hero, Jesus, I was literally reborn in every way. No, I did not climb inside my mom and come back out again, but my life became so much better that it literally changed me into living a new life beyond all my wildest dreams.

My new reading skills changed my grades from Cs and Ds in grammar school into As and Bs in junior high school, and I discovered a strong interest and personal talent in all subjects based on science and mathematics. I had found the place where I belonged, and looking ahead even at such a young age, I could clearly see my life was heading straight into a career in mathematics and science. Furthermore, because of my intense and growing fascination with all kinds of radios, I was sure my future career would in some way be the development of bigger and more powerful radios. To this end, I took two important steps into the future. I first studied for, and passed, an FCC license exam for amateur radio operation, which included the privilege to both transmit and receive distant shortwave radio signals, and I began competing in my school's science fair. Soon, I was contacting other amateur (i.e. ham) radio operators around the world. This was a time long before the internet, personal computers, or cell phones, so it was very special to have gained the ability to contact other ham stations in faraway places like Russia and France using radio equipment I had built myself.

Like it was yesterday, I can still remember my first science fair project. I purchased a postage stamp-sized solar cell from a mail order catalog and connected it to a small electric motor with a plastic propeller attached to its shaft. A small desk lamp rounded out my project. When the light was turned on, the solar cell produced an electric current that started the motor turning and the propeller spinning around. Within this simple demonstration was a sustainable energy source (the light provided by my desk lamp), which produced mechanical energy to turn a propeller that could potentially drive a ship or an airplane.

For its time (the 1950s), my project pointed toward the future by providing a simple demonstration of a sustainable energy source for powering the cars, boats, and airplanes of the future. My science project was such a success that the principal of my school asked if I would explain what I had done to the whole student body, which was gathered each week for an assembly. That's not the kind of request you turn down lightly. I had to say yes, but I was scared to death.

The day of the assembly came, and as I started talking, I heard a strange knocking sound under the podium. I realized it was my knees knocking together. I prayed for courage, and I was not disappointed. Much to my surprise and relief, I discovered that I had a talent for public speaking and speaking without notes. It reminded me of how my hero, Jesus, told his friends that when the situation demanded it, they would be granted the right words at the right time by the Holy Spirit. To this day, I never use any notes when speaking publicly. This talent may be a positive result of my earlier brush with dyslexia. Before my born-again experience, written notes would have been useless to me as a nonreader. After I learned to read, the pattern was established, and I never again considered writing down notes or using them during a speech.

When I advanced to high school, I won many state and regional science fair awards. These awards brought me lots of public attention, including radio and TV show appearances, and a local TV station even brought a mobile news crew out to my home and interviewed me in the living room as my mom looked on adoringly. I was hoping that all of this attention and publicity made up in some way for the pain and anguish my mom had suffered because of my reading problems before my born-again experience.

At school, I soon found out I was receiving loving treatment from my teachers, which was big a switch from grammar school when my teachers found me to be a problem student who refused to apply himself adequately. In fact, my chemistry teacher made a private laboratory available for me to use for building the latest year's science fair project. He even gave me a key, so no one else could get in and damage my yet to be completed project.

My high school grades were very high, and I had no trouble getting accepted at all of the colleges I applied to during senior year. I choose to attend Worcester Polytechnic Institute, a small science and engineering college just west of Boston. After four years, I graduated with a BS degree in electrical engineering, having maintained the same high grade point average as I had in high school. My professors all urged me to go on to graduate school and suggested that I consider Cornell or Stanford. Since I really didn't want to move all the way to California, Cornell seemed to be the right choice.

Since it was the time of the Vietnam war, I suffered through a number of nervous moments as my draft board alternately reclassified me from student deferment to 1A (i.e. ready to be drafted). My hero must have been taking care of me, because, thank heavens, I was never called up. I started graduate school at Cornell in the fall after my college graduation.

Cornell offered me to opportunity to broaden my education to include—in addition to electrical engineering—study in my minor fields of physics and applied physics. I became part of an organization called the "Microwave Center," which drew both students and faculty from electrical engineering, physics, applied physics, and material science. I completed a master's degree in a year and a half, and I was asked to join a PhD program if I was interested.

My dad was skeptical about the PhD program because he found it hard to understand why I would want to remain a poor student with all those high-paying engineering jobs being offered to me. After some difficult discussions, I told him that even though I was still a poor student, the School of Electrical Engineering paid my tuition and paid me a meager stipend that kept my body and soul together. I didn't think my PhD would take much longer, and it didn't. I graduated with a PhD degree in less than two years. My PhD thesis topic was "A Study of Oscillator Noise in GaAs Gunn Diodes," and my thesis topic helped launch me into my first job out of graduate school. My initial on-the-job design was a truly low-phase noise, ultra-frequency stable, local oscillators for "long lines" long-distance telephone service, which helped my company launch a new manufacturing product line.

Over the years, I have had many interesting jobs, resulting in many technical publications, many patents (more than fifteen), and many awards, speeches, and invited technical papers, including the 1977 IEEE MTT Microwave Prize, which I shared with two collogues. The Microwave Prize is the highest award in the microwave electronics field and is a great honor to receive. During this period, I published two books on integrated circuit design at microwave frequencies. Along the way, my designs have served to help start up six small companies as they prepared for their initial product offerings. Today, many of these companies are successfully growing their businesses in places like Korea, China, Taiwan, Japan, and the United States.

In the early 1990s, I served as the technical program chairperson for a conference in Santa Clara, California, which focused on converting military microwave electronics technology into its commercial equivalents. This conference was held just before the start of the cellular telephone revolution, and it served as a prophecy for what was coming next.

For the past twenty years, in addition to working at my engineering consulting practice, I have been teaching at Santa Clara University in Santa Clara California. Also, for the past four years, I have been the principle investigator for a research project studying the unique properties of certain garnet crystal resonators at the Nanotechnology Center of the Lawrence Berkeley National Laboratories. My project deals with investigating very special garnet crystals for applications to the latest generation of cellular phones.

Over the past fifty years, my deep and abiding interest in science has been complemented by my similar deep and abiding interest in spirituality. To this end, I have written two previous books, *The Unity of Truth: Solving the Paradox of Science and Religion* (Allen A. Sweet, C. Frances Sweet, and Fritz Jaensch, iUniverse 2012) and *A Little Book of Meditations* (Allen A. Sweet and C. Frances, iUniverse 2018).

New Wine Skins is my third spirituality book, and I have also published and spoken widely in the field of the "science-religion" dialogue. My 2015 contribution to the Journal of the Center for Theology and Natural Science in Berkeley's special event publication of Stuart Kauffman's concept of the "cosmic mind" was called a "Response to Stuart Kauffman: The Paradox of Divine Action and Scientific Truth" by Allen A. Sweet, C. Frances Sweet, and Fritz Jaensch.

Along the way, I earned a bachelor's degree in theological studies from the Episcopal Dioceses of California's School for Deacons, and I accompanied my wife Fran on her journey toward ordination. Fran and I went to classes all day Saturday each week, and sometimes on weekday evenings.

The Deacons program lasted three years and turned out to be one of the greatest joys of my life. It is a very small school (forty or fifty students), and we all got to be very close. It is hard not to get close to your brother and sister students when each week we all would bare our souls about how difficult our lives can become. In spite of the fact that we were only together for one day a week, as the days turned into weeks and the weeks turned into months, I started to realize that, for the first time in my life, I had become part of a Christian community. I will never forget that feeling. The experience opened up my understanding of what Jesus's kingdom of God might be about. When graduation came, and all of my newly ordained classmates wore their clerical collars for the first time, I began to realize that this wonderful phase in my life was coming to an end—perhaps never to be repeated. I felt a certain sadness as the curtain came down on our school days. I told myself that I had papers to publish and books to write and should be looking to the future.

Many church friends asked me during this time if I was interested in pursuing ordination, but I told them that I believe God is calling me to be a scientist and not a minister. I don't think I could do both. Maybe I was right, and maybe I was wrong. Whatever the case, my experience of being a part of a Christian community for three years will always live lovingly within my heart.

The book that follows discusses the origins and significance of human emotions. As we shall see, who we are is largely determined by the emotions we carry within our hearts. Jesus's four Gospels have a high emotional content. About half of this book is a commentary on how we, living in a scientific age two thousand years later, can view and understand the emotional content of Jesus's words within the four Gospels. Within the commentaries, each occurrence of an emotion within Jesus's words is noted, discussed, and explained in ways that are consistent with our twenty-first century scientific thinking and ideas. It is our emotions that qualify us for a place in God's kingdom, which Jesus came to establish.

Introduction

The purpose of this book is to present readers everywhere a comprehensive explanation of Jesus's teachings in a way that is consistent with the understandings of modern science and true to the core teachings that Jesus presented in the four Canonical Gospels (Matthew, Mark, Luke, and John). This is a discussion of how Jesus's kingdom of God could be established within our scientific world in ways that have not been successful within historic churches.

The core concepts that are addressed by the book are who Jesus is and who we are. First and foremost, Jesus is God! First and foremost, we are human beings known best by our emotional makeups. As we shall see, Jesus came first to found his kingdom of God on earth and, like a physician, save us from the emotional diseases that plague us all. Jesus didn't have much time in which to act because, as he knew well, the world of his day was not ready for him or his teaching. Once people began to notice him and listen to his teaching, the end was near because of all the invested interests that needed to kill him. But the work of building the kingdom lives on, and so do Jesus's teachings. Today is a new day within our scientific world, which is now two thousand years after Jesus's time. Perhaps Jesus will now be heard as his work and teachings are presented to our world within their new wine skins.

For nearly two thousand years, Christians worldwide have believed that Jesus is God and that Jesus's words (in his four Canonical Gospels) are God's own words. It has been more than two thousand years since Jesus walked the earth, and a lot has changed since Jesus's time. The whole of modern scientific thought has come about during the past four hundred years. The people of Jesus's time were totally unaware of concepts like geology, chemistry, mechanics, electromagnetism, thermodynamics, the evolution of species and natural selection, emotional psychology, quantum mechanics, and general relativity. These scientific disciplines have greatly colored how the people of our time view life on our earth and in our universe.

The great scientist Albert Einstein once was asked if science and religion were natural opposites. Einstein answered, "Absolutely not, they support each other, without science, religion is blind, and without religion, science is lame" (see *The Unity of Truth*).

Einstein doesn't sound like an atheist in any way, but on the other hand, he may not have been very comfortable with any of the traditional religious paths. Einstein's scientific work brought him such a high degree of satisfaction with his own approach to finding the truth that science and religion merged and become as one for him.

Like Einstein, it is hard for all of us living in the age of science to consider following a religion that does not involve the important concepts of science in some very significant ways. To ask people to turn off their scientific understanding before entering a church is completely unreasonable. To make religion (Christianity in this case) meaningful to the people of our day, at least some of the most important scientific concepts must be introduced as an integral part of religion. This book explores how scientific ideas might be introduced into Christianity in a way that Jesus's words would take on a new and real meaning for the scientifically aware.

Thomas Jefferson once took a copy of the Bible and used a shaving razor to remove all references to events that were "magical" to him, including Jesus's healings, exorcisms, walking on water, and raising people from the dead. Jefferson's intention was to reduce Jesus's Gospel references to only the references that involved his ethical teachings. However, the material that Jefferson chose to remove was the very material that made Jesus seem special, wholly believable, and creditable in the sense that he spoke unerringly for God the Father. Jefferson may have felt that removing the material was freeing the Gospels from the grip of superstition, but in fact, he was bringing into question the most important premise of the Gospels: Jesus and God and one and the same.

Two thousand years ago, people in the Middle East lived a kind of pastoral lifestyle by growing wheat and grapes and raising sheep and cows. In those times, it was natural for Jesus to draw analogies, in the form of parables, to use people's everyday experiences in their agriculture lives as he explained his theology. Two thousand years later, our lives are very different. We now live in an age when science and logic are the chief factors that color how we view the world and universe. The agricultural analogies of Jesus's day don't ring true anymore for most of us. Our thinking is so colored by the findings and philosophy of science that we need to structure our theological analogies along scientific lines if they are to be believable for people in our time. This book explores this possibility by first accepting the validity of every "jot and title" that Jesus spoke but recasting his words into a framework of scientific understanding that can be fully understood by the people of our age.

Jesus spoke often of healing people who were living under the control of devils and evil spirits. In our day, we think of these people as having given over their emotional control to their "selfish" evolutionary-based emotions, such as anger, hate, fear, and greed, all of which reside encoded within our body's DNA as the result of thousands of years of the evolutionary natural selection process. The healing that Jesus brings to these people is, by the grace of God, the emotional replacement or redemption of selfish emotions by God's own virtues.

The selfish emotion or emotions that were previously controlling the individual are replaced by their "mirror image dual" emotions derived from God's own virtues. Jesus brings to us love replacing hate, patience replacing anger, courage replacing fear, and generosity replacing greed. God, in Jesus, offers us the redemption of replacing our selfish emotions with God's own virtues. It takes faith in Jesus, and God the Father within him, to accomplish this emotional redemption when we open ourselves to accepting his healing power. For most of us, this process involves the extensive use of creative dreaming, meditation, and prayer over a long period of time. Within my own personal experiences, the process, by prayer and meditation, of changing my pride into humility took many months of concentrated effort. In a similar way, my personal efforts to change fear into courage took months and years of effort since the particular dreams that brought me healing redemption came on their own schedule and not on mine. This work goes on.

Chapter 1

Who Is God?

God is the name Christians, Jews, and Muslims give to the unnamable eternal reality of unlimited possibilities. God was here long before the creation of our universe, and God will still be here long after the destruction of our universe. God is everything and nothing, all at the same time. Nothing is beyond God's creative capabilities. With God, everything is possible. God's reality extends from the grandest and greatest to the smallest and the humblest. Creativity is one of the names we might choose to give God, but like all names we could choose for God, it falls far short of describing God's ultimate reality. God does not so much create in a human sense; instead, God shepherds and guides his creations into being in a slow and never-ending process of change and refinement, sometimes over very long periods of time.

God does not speak our language, and we do not speak God's language! God is not bound in any way by human reason and logic, and we cannot comprehend God's reason and logic. God's plan is not our plan, and our plan may or may not be a part of God's plan. We perceive God both within ourselves as the internal God within our hearts and outside of ourselves as the external God revealed to us by science. When we listen for God, we listen in places beyond all words, logic, and reason.

Our best listening tools for our internal God are silence, inspiration, meditation, prayer, music, poetry, dance, and art. Our best listening tools for the external God are the ever-evolving and ever-expanding concepts of modern science. Each of our own personal emotional makeups is closely related to our experience of the internal God. It is through our emotions that God helps shape our beings in ways that draw us closer to him. We are all unique individuals, and our uniqueness is defined first and foremost by our own emotional makeup.

Chapter 2

Emotional Duality

We are all dualists—even if we don't believe it or don't know what the word *dualist* really means. Our two sides are first, the emotional makeup we have inherited from the evolutionary process that produced us, and second, we are the sum total of all our thoughts, experiences, concerns, wonderments, longings, and speculations, all of which make us truly human.

You might say the genetic coding we inherit from our ancestors (both human and animal) is the blueprint for how our bodies are built and how we are to behave in any number of difficult and challenging situations. Of course, it is evolution's prime directive that in order for us to distribute our genetic material as widely as possible within the gene pool of our species, we as individuals must survive for as long as possible and produce as many offspring as we possibly can during our lifetimes. Evolution's prime directive drives the natural selection process forward.

Evolution's prime directive exists for the sole purpose of spreading our genes throughout our species' gene pool, assuming that we, as individuals, have received a genetic mutation making us more fit to confront and survive in the challenging environment we find ourselves living in today. These successful mutations become encoded within our bodies in order to ensure us, and our genetic offspring, longer lives within the particular environment we live in. A kind of positive feedback process occurs that causes successful mutations, when they occur, to spread rapidly throughout our species' gene pool. In a similar way, unsuccessful mutations die out quickly and are quickly removed from the gene pool.

Each of us as human beings (worldwide) are subject to the same selfish emotions—fear, greed, anger, hate, lust, jealousy, envy, pride, lying, vengefulness, suspicion, and judgment—that have been planted within our species' genome throughout eons of evolution. While these emotions certainly have their place within our lives—for instance, fear may sound a warning of impending disaster—we do not consider them to be the "be all and end all" of who we are as loving, caring human beings. In fact, a very long list of God's own virtues stand in direct contradiction to our selfish emotions.

To list God's virtues, simply name the opposite of each selfish emotion: love, trust, faith, courage, generosity, patience, love, affection, magnanimousness, humility, forgiveness, compassion, and truthfulness. If you are a believing Christian, you will immediately recognize this list of virtues as the way of being that Jesus taught his disciples and anyone else who would listen to him: Love your neighbor as yourself. Love your enemies and forgive your neighbor as God forgives you. The devil will promise you the world, but accepting his promise may destroy you. A man with murder in his heart has already killed someone. Forgive and forget. Have faith that the seeds you sow will be made to grow by God. Trust in God to care for you, and you will be forgiven by God's grace should you fall off the path of virtue.

By following Jesus's advice, it becomes clear that every selfish emotion within us can be countered by an alternative virtue. This is the duality of human selfish emotions versus God's virtuous emotions (Jesus speaking as God). The two exist simultaneously as opposite sides of the same coin. They are very much a part of each other; for instance, without the existence of fear, courage would be meaningless. Without greed, there would be no sense of generosity. Without blame, there would be no sense of forgiveness. We must accept the simultaneous existence of both sides of our emotional coins; our raw selfish emotions are on one side of our emotional coins, and their emotional twin, God's own virtues, are on the other. Without this full complement of our two emotional states within us, we would not be human beings.

All human conflicts originate within the seeming contradiction between our two dualistic emotional sides. God, in Jesus, offers us the virtues we long to embrace, but our evolutionary past pulls us back down into the selfishness from the eons of our ancestors experiencing fight-or-flight situations in the kill-or-be-killed world of genetic evolution.

In the end, it is always our decision, and ours alone, to act in a self-centered, selfish way based on our evolutionary past or to embrace the Godly virtues that Jesus is offering us. This is the nature of our

God-given gift of free will. It is always our choice to make, and most of us slide back and forth from one side of the emotional coin to the other in the emotional choices we make.

Only God is perfect, but human beings who strive to embrace the Godliness of virtue are constantly being pulled and tugged back and forth. It is like we are constantly being exposed to the sales pitch of an expert salesperson, which we are! Remember the story of Adam and Eve and the snake in the book of Genesis? It is here that we need God's help most and his forgiveness in particular. It is so easy for us to slip and slide down an emotional slope of utter selfishness, and when things get really out of hand, feel God will never forgive us—but God will! God always wants us back—no matter how far we slide backward into our selfish emotions and away from God's call to embrace his virtues.

We remember Jesus's parable of the prodigal son. No matter how many mistakes the son makes, the father always loves him and wants him back. Like in all of Jesus's parables, the key to understanding is knowing who is playing what role. In this parable, the father is God the Father, and the son is all of us at our worst.

CHAPTER 3

Evolution

In order to work effectively, evolution requires the appearance of mutations as agents of change. When Charles Darwin stopped at the Galapagos Islands during his 1835 around-the-world survey expedition, he was amazed to find little finches on each of the Galapagos Islands that were perfectly adapted to eating the food resources available on their particular island. Their beaks and claws seemed to be specially crafted to grasp and crack open the particular berries and seeds growing on their island. When Darwin moved on to the next island, he found the finches on this island were also perfectly adapted in beak and claw to eat the special berries and seeds found on *their* particular island.

On his way back to England, Darwin thought the finches hadn't been created by God so much as the finches must have "designed" themselves to be perfectly suited to living life on their own particular island. This was when concepts like the evolution of species and natural selection began to occur to Darwin. Surely, these islands were too far from the mainland of Peru for new little finches to fly out from the mainland, meaning the process by which the finches became of the form they are today must have happened a long time ago on their own little island. It was at this point that Darwin began to think much more carefully about the whole idea of mutations and natural selection.

Of course, in Darwin's day, there was no knowledge of genetics—amazingly, Charles Darwin and Augustinian friar Gregor Johann Mendel, the father of genetics, lived at the same time and were surprisingly unaware of each other's work—let alone the quantum mechanical concepts that underpin the understanding of all genetic mutations. All that Darwin knew for certain was that certain traits could be passed down from the parents to their children. However, in a few very special cases, the offspring developed special and entirely new traits, making them particularly well suited for a life in the environment they were born into. These new traits granted to the parent who receives a successful mutation, lucky offspring with similar new traits, perhaps leading to longer and more successful lives than their parents had experienced.

Of course, a longer life leads to more offspring. Over time, these new and successful traits would spread throughout the entire gene pool of the species. We now understand these improved traits to be a result of spontaneous modifications to an individual's DNA. Spontaneous DNA modifications are called mutations and may be as simple as swapping out a single base pair (one of four possible) of genetic information within the DNA molecule. The process is very similar to the way the ones and zeros of a digital bit may be swapped out within a digital electronic memory device such as a computer.

The cause of a genetic mutation is not always clear, but it is thought in most cases to result from cosmic rays, or some other forms of radiation, which impact the DNA molecules within the sperm or egg cell of a parent. Of course, whenever radiation is involved, the resulting mutations are subject to the laws of quantum mechanics, meaning that God's non-causal communications (see *The Unity of Truth,*) are being carried out in the form of quantum interactions, clearly pointing to the hand of God playing a role in the creation of genetic mutations.

It also suggests that God's hand has a role to play, not as a designer, but as a guide or a shepherd, in bringing about the genetic modifications to species, including ourselves. Therefore, we can think of God's role in the evolutionary process as one of slowly and patiently guiding a species through changes in response to both environmental changes and God's evolving plan for a particular species. We recognize that God's role in the evolutionary process as always being that of a shepherd and never a designer.

Chapter 4

Theories on Evolution since Darwin

Darwin did not have the last word on the subject of evolution. Many researchers since Darwin's time have made new contributions to this fascinating field. Most of these works are based on the human dilemma of raising a human baby to adulthood. This process, including the all-important education period, takes nearly twenty years.

A twenty-year commitment of time and resources to make the child-rearing project a success cannot be overstated. It is an impossible job for the mother of the child to do alone, and she must depend on family and friends to support her in all ways. First and foremost, within her support network, must be the father. Most cultures strongly urge—and some legally require—fathers to remain committed to the mother both in terms of financial and time commitments. Many of the more recent evolutionary theories, including Darwin own theory in *The Descent of Man*, have rooted their theories deep in the soil of the human child-rearing dilemma.

However, the origins of the selfish emotions discussed in much of this book go much further back into evolutionary history than the relatively recently period of dealing with raising human children over a twenty-plus-year commitment of time and resources. The origins of our selfish emotions, such as hate, fear, anger, and greed, go much further back in evolutionary history to the time of fight-or-flight" and kill-or-be-killed. The human brain is a "layered organ" and its composition is the creation of layers from our most ancient ancestors right up to the prefrontal cortex regions contributed by our more recent human predecessors. However, the origins of the more ancient regions of the human brain (the deepest layers) go back to early human, or pre-human time periods, which contribute most intensely to our selfish emotions.

We are who we are, but with God's help, we can and do find ways to replace the selfish emotions of our bodies with the virtuous emotions of our spirit, which are offered to us by God.

My friend Dasher Keltner is a professor of psychology at the University of California in Berkeley. For many years, Dasher has worked in the field of scientifically measuring and theorizing about the nature of human emotions. In 2009, Dasher wrote a wonderful book, *Born to be Good: The Science of a Meaningful Life*, which points out that Charlies Darwin himself was among the first scientists to explore the possibility that evolution itself might possibility account for some of our positive emotions, such as sympathy and compassion.

In 1878, Darwin's *The Descent of Man* suggested that sympathetic individuals were more successful in raising healthier offspring to adulthood and reproductive age. Therefore, Darwin theorized that sympathetic individuals were "themselves" capable of getting more of their own genetic material into the gene pool in a way that did not require mutations—only an inclination toward sympathy, kindness, and compassion to be passed on to their children. For Darwin, sympathy was one of our strongest instincts, and Darwin felt that sympathy likely served as the foundation of all human ethical systems. However, many scientists after Darwin's time did not embrace sympathy as a leading product of the evolutionary process, and his concept has died out, until fairly recently.

Professor Keltner next explored the possibility that compassion may have a biological basis within the human body and brain. Chris Ovies, a former student of professor Keltner's, was said by professor Keltner to have staked his career on the concept that the vagus (means wandering in Latin) nerve being the wellspring of all human sympathy and compassion. The vagus nerve meanders through the chest cavity from the very top of the spinal column and connects the facial muscles with most of the internal organs, including the liver, the kidneys, the intestines, and the stomach. In certain particularly gifted individuals, the vagus nerve seems to slow down heart and respiration rates and bring about a general feeling of warmth and tranquility that spreads across the subject's entire chest area. Certain individuals who are especially talented in terms of their vagus nerve responses associate the cause of their own feelings of sympathy and compassion with the results of their vagus nerve's stimulation. Other less talented individuals may see little connection between the stimulation of their vagus nerve and their own feelings of sympathy, caring, and compassion.

My own opinion is that if the vagus nerve is truly the biological location of our feelings of sympathy, caring, and compassion, it is likely that with serious ongoing prayer and mediations, we can ask God to grant us these virtuous emotions by allowing us to experience the stimulation of our vagus nerve. If God made our bodies, then God can influence our bodies.

Interestingly, the vagus nerve only occurs in mammals and not in reptiles or other creatures. Perhaps the vagus nerve was included in mammalian bodies because God foresaw the need in mammals to experience sympathy, caring, and compassion to ease the parenthood demands placed on all mammals (and humans in particular).

Professor Keltner has also done considerable work on facial expressions as displays of our emotions. As noted above, a direct neural connection exists between the vagus nerve and our facial muscles. Human beings seem to be wired for emotional expression in so many different ways. This realization leads me to feel that who we really are in our heart of hearts can be summed up by the emotions that reside there. We may not all wear our hearts on our sleeves, but we all surely wear our emotions on our faces.

In his 1975 book *Sociobiology,* E. O. Wilson of Harvard wrote that social behaviors, such as altruism, can be programed by evolution into a species to help its survival. Wilson later enlarged the theory to include *kin selection,* which favors people who share genetic relationships to pass along altruisms such as compassion and sympathy.

In 2010, Wilson backtracked on his kin selection theory because his further research, along with that of his Harvard colleagues, convinced him that altruism arises not for the good of the genes but for the good of the community! Wilson had come to feel the real point was that groups that cooperate ultimately dominate groups that don't cooperate. This means altruism arises not to protect families (kin) but to protect social groups (kin or not). Based on Wilson's ideas, it seems that no direct evolutionary path exists producing altruism in genetically related individuals. Once again, the role of introducing altruism to the individual remains the domain of religion!

However, a fascinating development was published in the journal *Brain* in 2012 by a team of researchers at the Mount Sinai School of Medicine in New York City. These researchers identified a region of the human brain called the *anterior insular cortex,* which they proved to be the center in the brain where human empathy originates. The anterior insular cortex is located in a hidden region deep within the brain. Perhaps the meaning of this discovery to the present work is to demonstrate that some kind of evolutionary process must have been underway to produce a biological region within the human brain that is responsible for human empathy—in a way that is very similar to what Keltner and Ovies associate with the vagus nerve (see above).

Certain tie-ins have been identified between a limited number of emotions and certain locations within the brain. For instance, fear is connected with the hypothalamus and the amygdala. Sadness is connected to the hippocampus and the right occipital lobe. Anger is connected to the hippocampus and the amygdala. These connections seem to be distributed to a number of different brain locations, and in some cases, the same brain location is connected with more than one emotion. It is likely that identifying the emotional responses associated with certain brain locations is still in its infancy.

Finally, Sarah Blaffer Hrdy, of Harvard—with the most recent approach of her work taken in *Mothers and Others: The Evolutionary Origins of Mutual Understanding*—offers a second look at the meaning of being human. If, as Hrdy proposes, humans have thrived by cooperative breeding, a child-rearing strategy requiring networks of individuals to help in raising healthy children, many of our more individualistic views of who we are as human beings may now be in question.

Chapter 5

Scientific Duality

The Time-Frequency Duality of Fourier's Theorem

In about 1620, the philosopher and future scientist Rene Descartes was a young mercenary fighting in southern Germany during the Thirty Years' War. As the story goes (it may in reality be a scientific myth), Descartes spent a night in a ceramic furnace (perhaps some type of sauna bath?) where he fell into a trance and experienced many strange dreams. Chief among them was a strong prediction that mathematics was destined to become the language of science, thereby revolutionizing the futures of all the natural sciences.

When Descartes awoke in the morning, he became convinced that his dreams were more than mere nonsense and that they were in fact a prophecy of science's future, which they truly were! Albert Einstein once remarked that the greatest of all scientific mysteries is why mathematics is even capable of, not to mention so successful at, describing the operations of nature.

During the two hundred years following Descartes's lifetime, many brilliant mathematicians lived and gained recognition in France, Germany, and elsewhere. One of greatest of these mathematical geniuses was Joseph Fourier. He lived in France between 1768 and 1830. Fourier's most famous work was known as Fourier's theorem, which concerns the mathematical description of periodic time functions and waves. Fourier showed by mathematical analysis that periodic time functions could be expressed as either functions of time or functions of frequency (frequency is defined as one over the time period of a periodic function). It didn't matter whether a periodic function was being expressed within the time domain or within the frequency domain, the results would be exactly the same, but the two descriptions appear on their face to be quite different. However, because of the unique nature of time functions and the unique nature of frequency functions, Fourier was able to show that it was necessary to express any periodic function as both a time domain function and a frequency domain function for achieving a complete understanding of the usefulness of a particular periodic function's properties. Therefore, we would say that a time-frequency duality exists within the mathematical world of Fourier's periodic functions.

To fully understand the meaning of Fourier's periodic functions, it is necessary to understand the behavior of the periodic function in both its time domain form and in its frequency domain form. Anything less (any limit on either our understanding of the function's time domain behavior or its frequency domain behavior) will seriously limit our ability to understand a periodic function's usefulness over its full range application.

Since most of the mathematical expressions used in modern physics and engineering are periodic functions, the time-frequency duality of Fourier's theorem has served as the mathematical underpinning of most of modern physics, including such important phenomena as electromagnetic wave theories, vibrating mechanical structures, and quantum wave mechanics. In engineering, this mathematical underpinning extends to the electrical circuits that give rise to all the technological wonders of integrated circuits and information processing. Fourier's theorem is responsible for initially creating the need to understanding why dualities exist at all within the many of the branches of science.

Light as a Duality

In 1905, Albert Einstein was working as a low-paid patent assistant at a patent law office in Bern, Switzerland. Since his work required his full attention for only four hours a day, and he was employed for eight hours a day, with his boss's blessing, Einstein used the remaining four hours to explore his own pet physics theories. This extra four hours was a great gift to Einstein. He desperately wanted to devote his life to an academic career, but to move ahead, he needed to find a willing professor to chair his doctoral committee. Einstein's plan was to publish one or two technical papers and gain recognition by sending these papers to a number of the more well-known physics professors at German-speaking universities. It was Einstein's amazing good fortune to have gained those extra four hours per day because those extra four hours turned out to make Einstein an esteemed scientist who changing our world forever.

Einstein's first and his best paper, which ultimately led to his Nobel Prize in 1927, was based on explaining the enigma of a recent physics experiment called the *photoelectric effect*. The experimental setup for the photoelectric effect was as follows: A controllable beam of light was shined onto a metal bar (perhaps platinum). The beam of light would "knock" electrons out of the metal bar. The energy of the emitted electrons was measured by an associated particle detector. When the light beam's intensity was turned up to full brightness, the energy of the emitted electrons remained unchanged. However, when the color of the light (by adjusting the color of the light source from red to violet) was "tuned" across the full range of colors, the energy of the emitted electrons was changed from the lowest electron energies appearing with red light and the highest electron energies appearing with violet light. In fact, a straight-line relationship existed between the energies of the emitted electrons and frequency (i.e. color) of the light at a slope that was exactly equal to Planck's constant (6.63E-34 J-sec). At the time, no existing physical theory was capable of explaining the behavior observed in the photoelectric effect, creating what had become a great scientific mystery that Einstein was about to solve!

Einstein's solution to the mystery was both simple and profound. He explained that Isaac Newton had theorized back in the 1690s that light existed as a cloud of particles that is experienced by our eyes as a spectrum of colors, depending upon the speed of the individual particles. Newton's explanation held up well for nearly two hundred years, until the Scottish physicist James C. Maxwell published his famous paper combining all of the electric and magnetic mathematical relationships into a single set of four equations bearing Maxwell's name. Maxwell's equations demonstrated that all electromagnetic energy radiates as waves—regardless of frequency. Therefore, what we call radio waves, infrared waves, light waves, and x-rays are all understood to be of the same kind of electromagnetic wave phenomenon, operating at different frequencies. Scientists worldwide quickly embraced Maxwell's wave theory of light and put Newton's light particle concepts out with the trash!

Einstein's solution to the photoelectric experiment enigma was simple, elegant, and revolutionary! Einstein simply stated that Newton and Maxwell were both correct! Einstein's proposal was that light could only be understood as a wave-particle duality. As Einstein saw it, light was only comprehensible as being simultaneously a particle, which he called a photon, and an electromagnetic wave described by Maxwell's equations. The energy of the photon particle was exactly calculated to be Planck's constant (6.63E-34 J-sec) times the frequency of the wave.

To fully comprehend the meaning of light, Einstein proposed that one must simultaneously understand both its wave nature and its particle nature! There was no way that the two natures could be separated; they both existed as part of a unified whole that we simply call light.

Within months, researchers in France had performed similar experiments to the photoelectric effect, proving that in the same way light was simultaneously both a wave and a particle, particles (such as electrons) were simultaneously both a particle and a wave! Much of the then established wisdom of physics had now been overturned as scientists around the world were being forced to grapple with an understanding of what it means for *all* matter and energy to exist simultaneously in the form of wave-particle dualities. It is out of this quest for understanding and the appreciation of the proper role of the wave-particle duality that the new science of quantum mechanics was born.

Wave-Particle Duality

As Einstein saw it, the wave nature of light was clearly described by Maxwell's electromagnetic equations; however, what describes the wave nature of particles such as electrons? The founders of quantum mechanics—Schrodinger, Heisenberg, Bohr, and Dirac—knew that something was "waving," but what was it?

Erwin Schrodinger proposed a universal quantum wave equation, which bears his name. He called the solutions to his wave equation a *wave function*, which turned out to be one of the strangest quantities ever to be proposed by physics. In fact, it is easier to make a list of what a wave function is not than to make a list of what a wave function *is*. A wave function is not measurable in the laboratory. A wave function is in general not a real number (i.e. wave function's amplitudes may be a mathematically complex number in the form of $A + iB$, where i is the square root of -1). A wave function has *no* straightforward physical interpretation. However, a wave function *is* a wave with all of the same wave-interference properties as any other wave (frequency, wavelength, phase, and wave reinforcement and cancellation). A wave function is both a function of time and a function of a three-dimensional position space. A wave function is "related" to the probability of finding a particle at some particular point in three-dimensional space at some particular point in time. A wave function is calculated based on knowing the particle's kinetic and potential energies.

As perplexing as it may seem, this quantum mechanical wave function has proven to be the key to understanding the secrets of subatomic world, leading to many, if not most, of the wonders of modern science and technology. The founders of quantum mechanics tried their best to find ways to theoretically separate a particle's "particle nature" from the particle's "wave nature" and *failed* in every attempt. Subatomic particles, like light, are fully understood only as a *duality*. Today, science is comfortable with accepting the reality of the wave-particle duality. All physical theories and laboratory measurements must take into account the reality of the wave-particle duality if the results are to be credible.

Chapter 6

Religious Dualities

Jesus as Fully Human and Fully Divine

In AD 381, a church council was held in Constantinople to settle leftover questions from an earlier church council held in Nicaea in AD 321. Chief among these questions was how to create a clear and definite statement about what the church believed to be the true nature of Jesus. The council concluded that Jesus was in fact fully human in every possible way and at the same time fully divine—completely God—in every possible way!

In effect, the Council of Constantinople concluded that Jesus was a "Human-God Duality." This statement represented a gigantic leap of faith in anyone's book. We would call this statement on Jesus's dual nature as defining his existence to simultaneously be both a human being and God. Like the subatomic entities of the quantum wave-particle duality, Jesus, as conceived by the Council of Constantinople could only be appreciated as being in every possible way a human being and being simultaneously in every possible way God! That must have been a shocking conclusion for the Christians of the day (and for many Christians in our day as well!), and it seemed to contradict all human logical thinking. However, we must assume that the gathered fathers of the church saw no alternative to drawing this conclusion since it is so utterly shocking. We assume the gathered church fathers faced up to a theology that led them to this shocking conclusion because any other conclusion would serve to either radically diminish Jesus's human nature or radically diminish Jesus's God nature. Either one of these would be seen as a serious questioning of how Jesus is described within the four Canonical Gospels. Such an impasse is truly the mark of a human-divine duality, which is Jesus.

The Duality of God's Unity and Diversity

When the people of the Roman Empire became Christian under the rule of Emperor Constantine, the emperor wanted to know what his subjects were expected to believe about their new faith. To this end, Constantine called a church council in AD 321 in the town of Nicaea (as mentioned above), which is located in what is now Turkey.

Constantine charged the church's leaders with producing a document containing a list of universal Christian beliefs. Chief among these beliefs was that God is first and foremost a unity (*Homoousios* in biblical Greek) and at the same time a diversity of three (*Hypostasis* in biblical Greek). Therefore, the council at Nicaea reached the conclusion that God's nature is truly a duality of perfect unity and a perfect diversity of three (i.e. the Trinity) at the same time!

Again, we see how completely the duality concept is woven into the warp and woof of Christianity at its most fundamental level. Never mind that such concepts make no sense to human understanding; we must always remain aware that God's understanding and human understanding are not the same! Those of us who live in the twenty-first century have already received a hint of the universal and God-given nature of dualities based on our scientific understanding of mathematical dualities, especially within the physics of quantum mechanics and its fundamental wave-particle duality.

We experience of God as an "Out-There" and at the Same Time an "In-Here" Duality.

God exists within each human being he created, but God also created the whole of the physical universe from its billions of galaxies to its myriad subatomic particles. We humans experience God as being inside of ourselves, God being inside other human beings, and God being within the whole of creation outside of human beings. Every blade of grass, every little animal or bird, every galaxy and every electron are part of God's creation.

There is no limit to God's creative abilities, and we humans are free to experience God in all places and in all forms at all times. God surely exists deep within the core of our very being, but God also exists deep within the core of every living and nonliving entity in the universe—all of which exists outside of ourselves.

During the self-examination of our prayers and meditations, we search for the "Inner God" who is inside us all. However, it is our scientific search outside of ourselves, to the very edges of the universe, that is our search for the "Outer God." Religious people primarily focus on searching for the "Inner God," but scientists focus primarily on the search for the Outer God. Both the Inner God and the Outer God *are* truly the same God, and they form an inner-outer duality of God, which is the only way that we humans can experience God. Many scientists are also religious, and many religious people are also scientists. In fact, the Outer God and the Inner God form the highest and most universal of all dualities. God only becomes fully accessible to us when we gain an appreciation for the concept that the Inner God and the Outer God, are in reality, the same God!

In terms of roles played by human beings, we can say that the full understanding of the God of the external world depends upon our scientific search for truth. At the same time, we can say that it is religion's role to search for and lead us to the goodness and virtue offered by our internal God.

CHAPTER 7

Our Emotional Duality and the Evolutionary Origins of Our Emotions

Our earliest animal ancestors led lives of survival of the fittest. They lived a "kill-or-be-killed" existence. When our earliest human ancestors appeared in the world, they moved around a lot. Our ancestors moved across the world in successive waves of migration. Many of our direct ancestors left their African homeland somewhere between 50,000 and 250,000 years ago and moved into what is now the Middle East. From there, our European and Asian ancestors split into two waves with many going northwest into Europe and many others going east into what is now Iran, Afghanistan, Pakistan, and India. Eventually, the eastward-moving group found its way into China, Korea, Japan, and Siberia. Eventually, some of those who came into Siberia moved across a land bridge into North America, during a particularly cold period in the earth's history when much of the ocean's water was frozen during an ice age. All along the way, our ancestors encountered other closely related indigenous human beings, such as the Neanderthal people who our ancestors first encountered in the Middle East and later in Europe.

Anthropologists regard the contact between our ancestors (*Homo sapiens*) and the indigenous Neanderthals as something of a mystery. One theory holds that since our ancestors, the *Homo sapiens*, had superior intelligence, superior strength, and superior weaponry than the Neanderthals, the indigenous Neanderthals were in effect "wiped out" by our ancestors. However, that may not be the case because the latest DNA research suggests that Neanderthals and *Homo sapiens* did mate on occasion, producing a race of hybrids who today are all of us.

In any case, it is likely that over many lifetimes, the indigenous Neanderthals were regarded by our *Homo sapiens* ancestors as being a vastly inferior underclass of sub-humans who were good for nothing except plunder and abuse. We reasonably expect that our *Homo sapiens* ancestors must have used every opportunity to steal, rape, murder, and enslave the poor Neanderthals. These experiences from the far distant past seemed to have trained *Homo sapiens* all over the world to become more self-centered, cruel, abusive, advantage taking, violent, warlike, and hateful. Our race does not present a very pretty picture over the longer span of history.

We have no way of knowing, but perhaps the indigenous Neanderthals they encountered were kind, generous, peaceful, and loving people. It is a fact that Neanderthal cave grave sites show evidence that mourners had left tributes of wildflowers on the bodies of the deceased. That does not sound like the behavior of a group of mindless, knuckle-dragging beasts. Wouldn't that be a switch! In the troubled age we live in now, perhaps if we knew the truth, we might want to bring back the Neanderthals!

Whatever actually happened during this period of early human history, it seems likely that evolutionary forces favored our race's tendency toward self-centered, violent, advantage-taking, and hateful behaviors. Our race has grown into just the kind of people who most desperately need God's forgiveness, redemption, and redirection. Our people were, and are, so in need of Jesus and all that he brings to us.

The Selfish Principle

There is little doubt that the evolutionary process has fitted us human beings with emotional dispositions that are in many ways selfish, cruel, and hateful. There is not a whole lot we can do about how evolution has shaped our being. We are who we are! If God can cry, he must be crying over us! It is always hard to watch your children go wrong. The list goes on seemingly without end: the wars, the racial hatred, the superweapons that threaten to wipe us out, the industrial pollution that makes a few people rich but chokes and poisons the rest of us, and the selfish uncaring that refuses to help others who are in such desperate need of help. Our utter selfishness is killing us all! As the cartoon character Pogo once said, "We have met the enemy and he is us!"

Free Will and Choice

Since the very beginning, God has granted us a precious gift: free will. Without free will, we would become mechanical automatons, slaves to some clearly deterministic principle. With the gift of free will, we have control over our own destinies and fates. We may freely choose as we wish. We may choose out of our own selfishness or embrace God's virtues. The choice is always ours alone. Even if we are making a terrible mistake, God will grant us the freedom to embrace the choices we have made—no matter how terrible the consequences.

Emotional Addiction

Like substance addiction, certain human personalities are inclined to repeat again and again their actions associated with experiencing certain selfish emotions. For example, someone who is inclined toward anger may on a regular basis be counted on to produce angry outbursts that frighten coworkers and family members alike. Why does he or she do this? The answer is deceptively simple: "It feels good." For some people, an angry explosion can be equivalent to drinking a double whiskey or shooting up heroin; for these people, the sensations associated with their angry outbursts yield unbelievably pleasure. Usually extreme anger is accompanied by pride and power within an unholy threesome that allows the one performing the outburst to experience the high of their thundering anger accompanied by a simultaneous rush of pride and power at having cowered their victim.

Many women experience this kind of emotional behavior from men with the added twist that, in their cases, lust is included in the emotional mix. The man, in effect, is saying, "Comply with my sexual demands if you know what is good for you." If the woman complies, the man gains the rush of his anger accompanied by his pride and power being fulfilled by dominating the woman, and as a frosting on the cake, he gets to enjoy the pleasure of sexual release. These kinds of emotional behaviors have given rise to the #MeToo movement, which unites all women who are being sexually abused by the powerful men who are forcing them to sexually do as they wish.

There are many examples of emotional addictions in literature. For example, Charles Dickens's *A Christmas Carol* is a tale of a man (Scrooge) who is deeply addicted to greed, and he makes all of his family and friends miserable as they watch his terribly selfish life wasting away. It is only with the intersession of several "spirits" that Scrooge finally comes to his senses and is redeemed on Christmas morning. *A Christmas Carol* has a happy ending, but the lives of many misers do not.

Another example is *Les Miserable,* in which an obsessed policeman tries until his very end to bring a kind and goodly man to justice for committing a petty crime. The addiction in this case is the policeman's obsession with being judgmental.

Shakespeare wrote several plays with themes of obsession and emotional addiction. In *The Merchant of Venice*, a loan shark demands the debtor promise, in case of default, to yield up a "pound of his flesh" to be taken from the debtor's heart. The debtor's attorney argues that mercy is a higher law than any payment-default agreement, and the loan shark has no right to take the poor debtor's life away in such a cruel and merciless way.

In another Shakespearian example, Lady Macbeth is so addicted to her notion of power and pride that she is driven to take the life of the king in order for her husband to replace him, making her queen.

In *Richard III*, we witness a king in the middle of a losing battle become de-horsed and surrounded by enemy troops, calling out to anyone who can hear him, "A horse, a horse, my kingdom for a horse," not realizing that his kingdom is now worthless and his life is truly at its end. However, he continues to trust in his prideful position as king, in which his power and pride had become his longstanding addiction.

A final example is a touching exchange between Jo and Marmee in Louisa May Alcott's *Little Women.* Jo tells Marmee she is often angry, and it is just the way she is, and there is nothing she can do about it no matter how hard she tries. Marmee then confides in Jo that she too is angry (at least once per day!), but even though she has tried hard to change, the best she has been able to do is keep her anger under control, so she won't inflict it on family and friends. Jo is shocked because she thinks of Marmee as being a consistently patient person with no angry tendencies at all. Marmee then tells Jo that her inability to rid her heart of anger, although she has gained control of her anger, is one of her greatest failings and the major disappointments of her life. You can't help feeling sorry for Marmee since she has struggled her whole life, trying to rid her heart of anger, but she can only get as far as controlling her anger when it threatens to overwhelm her. What a human tragedy!

It is also worth mentioning Herman Melville's *Moby-Dick*, which is the story of a fictional whaling ship captain. Ahab is obsessed with getting revenge on a white sperm whale that bit off his leg during a previous encounter. Ahab's maniacal revenge quest ends in the death of the entire ship's crew, including the captain.

No list of emotional addiction would be complete without mentioning Adolph Hitler's violent obsession with destroying the Ashkenazi Jews of Europe. Starting with the publication of *Mein Kampf* in the 1920s and concluding with the murder of more than three million Jews during World War II, Hitler's "insane hatred" of all Jews demonstrates how deeply one man's emotional addiction can be capable of plunging the entire world into horror and darkness.

The Grace of God-Given Emotional Alternatives

God's virtues are the alternative choices that we are granted, by God, to replace our own selfish emotions, which lie deep within our body's DNA. God's virtues exist on the other side of the emotional coin from our evolutionary-acquired emotions, which are based solely on our own selfish impulses.

The emotional choices we make determine what kind of people we are. Our personalities are like a patchwork quilt of up-and-down choices that we must make with our "emotional coins." The business of our lives is making these choices; some are easy to make, but others are very, very hard. In all cases, choosing God's virtues comes down to a precious gift from God. He freely offered us grace in order to help us escape the slavery of addiction, which imprisons us if we choose to follow only our own selfish, emotional choices.

As John Newton wrote nearly three hundred years ago in his famously loved song: "Amazing Grace, how sweet the sound, that saved a wretch like me, I once was lost but now am found, was blind but now I see."

Turning Over Our Coins

Let us picture our emotional coins on a chessboard. Some of the coins are selfish side up, and others are virtue side up. The board has to be quite large because life requires that we make a lot of choices over the course of our lives. We may find that whole areas of our board are consistently virtue side up, and other areas are exclusively selfish side up. The areas that are consistently selfish side up are in desperate need of correction. Does God allow us to rethink an emotional choice? You bet he does! In fact, God, in the form of Jesus, will help us make these changes. However, it isn't always easy for any of us to change.

In English, the word *redemption* means reclaiming an article by paying a price to get it back. Within Christianity, redemption refers to an act by God in which our sins are forgiven. However, there is a special sense of meaning in the word redemption that also implies that God must pay a price to get us back. For some Christians, the price of redemption is associated with the misery Jesus suffered as he hung dying on the cross. This concept is not a part of either Jesus's Gospels or the fourth-century founding creeds; it was proposed by Saint Anselm of Canterbury during the eleventh century.

Today, many Christians of all denominations adhere to this concept, which is called the "Satisfaction theory of atonement", but many other Christians find this proposal to be abhorrent. No Christian anywhere is required to believe this concept, but many do. However, many do not. I have never cared much for the satisfaction of theory of atonement, first and foremost because if we are truly saved only by the suffering of Jesus during his three agonizing hours on the cross, then why should we study and follow his teaching? Does this mean the teachings found in the four Gospels are of no value to us? I can't understand why this weakness in his concept did not occur to Saint Anselm before he published his theory. Surely, he was intimately familiar with the Gospels and all of their truths. How could he just turn his back on the necessity of learning and following the teachings of the Gospels, which for most of us has been a lifelong undertaking of study, prayer, and meditation. We previously discussed this problem in chapter 5 (i.e. the dying myth) in *A little Book of Meditations*.

An alternative idea to the satisfaction theory of atonement by Saint Anselm of Canterbury in the eleventh century CE) we could consider the origin of redemption to be based on the historic roots of the biological evolutionary process. Of course, since this material was not available to Saint Anselm for his comments, he will have to remain silent during the following discussion.

Like everything else in our universe, biological evolution is the product of God's creativity. However, there is a unique characteristic within evolution because the life forms that grow and change under evolution's influence must behave in a way that their own self-interests are carried out at all times; otherwise, natural selection will not work! Therefore, a "force of temptation" had to be built into this biological system to ensure that biological life forms are always inclined toward choosing their own self-interests under every circumstance.

With human beings, we simply call this driving force that pushes us toward satisfying our own self-interests "temptation," which we can personify into the "tempter." In Jesus's day, the tempter was call Satan or the devil. We remember from the Gospel accounts, Satan seemed to have high hopes of convincing Jesus to worship him during Jesus's forty days in the wilderness following his baptism. However, Satan was sadly disappointed to learn that Jesus refused to worship him and made it clear that he *only* worshiped God the Father. After many attempts on his part, Satan gave up and left Jesus alone, for now.

Fast-forward to the Crucifixion. Based on circumstances, Jesus was destined to be murdered—no matter what else happened. So many political and religious bullies wanted to kill him that he didn't stand a chance of survival. Even the Romans were beginning to take an interest in Jesus and regarded him as a troublemaker and a rabble-rouser.

The major assertion in the theory I am now stating is that when biological evolution first began, God granted some degree of spiritual independence to the tempter in order to make the evolutionary system work right. Since evolution is such a wonderful system for creating and modifying life forms, God may have felt reluctant to abandon his evolutionary process and choose to put up with the presence of a tempter.

Perhaps at the time of the Crucifixion, God suggested to the tempter that, based on his forty-day failure with Jesus, he could now take revenge by "having his way" with Jesus during the Crucifixion—if the tempter would agree to forever after stand aside while God granted redemption by grace to all people who followed Jesus's teachings and asked to have their emotional coins changed from their selfish side up to virtue side up. Of course, since Jesus was fully human and fully God, all the tempter could do to him was kill Jesus's human side during Jesus's agony on the cross, while Jesus's God side would return to the Father in heaven. On his way to heaven, Jesus briefly stopped by on Easter to say farewell to his disciples and his friends.

God must have taken this deal with the tempter in payment for redemption very seriously because, as we know from the book of Genesis, God had asked Abraham to sacrifice *his* son Isaac, and at the last minute, as Abraham was getting out the knife to kill Isaac, God made sure that a ram was caught in the bushes close by to substitute for Isaac as the sacrifice. However, God did not provide a ram as a substitute for Jesus—*his* own son—as Jesus died in agony on the cross. This deal of redemption must have been so important to God that he was willing to sacrifice his *own* son Jesus to make it happen, and we are the ones who benefit the most. This was truly divine love, and all believing Christian are its beneficiaries. Thank you, Jesus, for what you did to free us from the bondage of our own selfishness.

Within the concept of emotional duality, our emotions are carried out by making a choice between being selfish or being virtuous; it is very much like the choice made between a digital one and a digital zero that we associate with a bit of information in digital technology (hate versus love or fear versus courage). If we lead lives solely based on our own selfish emotions, we will likely engage in evil and commit sins. When we follow lives of virtue, our lives are filled with doing good works. As Jesus put it, we will be fruitful. In this role of living out virtue, we become role models for others.

When God redeems us, one or more of our emotional coins is upended within our hearts, and we become on the whole more virtuous and less selfish. God grants us this transformation based solely on his love for us, and he graces us with a gift that we could never pay for and don't deserve. This is not something we can achieve on our own; it is only accomplished through God's love and trust in us. However, we are required to ask God to grant our redemption through a process of prayer and meditation, which requires serious commitment on our parts.

When the act of redemption is accomplished, the particular emotion that is being upended reasserts itself as a virtue, and our lives become changed for all time. Right away, we notice how we have become more virtuous and less selfish. Again, we are reminded of the words of the song:

Amazing Grace how sweet the sound that saved a wretch like me, I once was lost, but now am found, was blind but now I see.

Chapter 8

Communications

How is it that we even know about God's virtues? We know about our selfish emotions simply because they are a part of our physical structure—they are encoded within our body's DNA—but how do God's virtues become a part of us? Virtues are not in any way a part of our physical makeup, but virtues are nonetheless part of who we really are. Is this simply a matter of learning and training since childhood? I think not! If we learn about virtue only from our parents and teachers, virtue would not be an eternal truth—and it would be far too easy for us to reject it out of hand.

In order for virtue to become grafted into the very core of our being, it must have a continuous ongoing presence within us at the very center of our being. Unlike our selfish emotions, virtue must constantly be refreshed and renewed (like the living waters that Jesus spoke about in the Gospels). Virtue is like a flowing stream that carries within its refreshing waters the knowledge that God is always calling on us to be there for others, to offer protection for the weak, and to offer a loving, kindly helping hand to all who stumble. For virtue to become an ongoing part of our lives, it must be constantly refreshed by means of a direct communication link to God, speaking to us at the very core of our being.

But how can this be? We are very sure that virtue is in no way encoded within our DNA because virtue does not in any way serve the survival goals of the evolutionary process (see chapters 3 and 4). None of the virtues will add even a second to our lifetimes. How do we learn about virtue in a way that can't be easily ignored? It is at this point that science comes to the rescue. In particular, quantum mechanics, the branch of physics that deals with the very small, offers us hints about how God can and does communicate directly to us. For greater details on these concepts, refer to *The Unity of Truth*.

The basis of God's direct communications with us lies within quantum mechanical non-causal events occurring at subatomic levels within our bodies. Within our bodies, information is constantly being processed and refreshed in ways that are not accessible to any kind of deterministic understanding. We may think of this spontaneous information as "just happening," seemingly without cause.

Subatomic events happen constantly within our bodies. The sum total of these events adds up to experiences such as dreams, intuitions, and the kind of mystical experiences that are associated with deep meditation and prayer. This may occur in moments of flashing insight of the kind religious people often report having while reading Holy Scripture. In any event, spiritual experiences such as these seemingly come out of nowhere and cannot be repeated later. They have no rational cause and cannot be summoned on demand.

Religious people call these events "workings of the Spirit" as God shares his Holy Spirit within us at these very special moments. Often, such events come to our rescue in times of crisis. A person finding himself or herself at a crossroads during a crisis may initially be tempted to take action, which is more consistent with one's own selfish emotional interests, but after taking a long walk or going to sleep for a while, the person may come around to a different point of view in determining a new course of action that is not selfish and contains a new element of virtue that he or she had not previously considered.

Virtue is always available to us—but not on demand. We must ask God for insight, but God will answer us in God's own way, in God's own time. However, it then becomes our responsibility to suspend our selfishness long enough for God to introduce us to the virtues we need to become aware of if we are to make the right decision to resolve our crisis. Prayer and meditation are often the keys to moving from emotional selfishness to virtue.

Virtue is from God and is pure Spirit. Those who have been redeemed lead lives of virtue and do good works. Selfishness is our inheritance from the evolutionary process of the past and is encoded deep within our bodies' DNA genetic codes. Selfishness is of the flesh. When we act out of selfishness, we serve evil and often commit sins.

In the Gospels, Jesus talks about the tempter (the devil) who tries to persuade us to follow our own self-serving ways. We must resist temptation; the Lord's Prayer says, "Lead us not into temptation but deliver us from evil." Mosaic law is concerned with avoiding evil acts (sins). Under the law, what is in one's heart is of little importance; it is the acts that a person commits that count.

On the other hand, virtue is wholly spiritual and resides within our hearts. Those who follow virtue are doers of good works. These people have been redeemed, their hearts are filled with virtue, and their lives are focused on doing good works. Since virtue has nothing to do with evil and sin, it exists outside of the workings of the law. However, it is the virtue that Jesus preached, and it is for the sake of virtue that we are redeemed by him.

CHAPTER 9

Antecedents to Jesus's Teachings

Several world religions and religious leaders between 700 BC and 300 BC promoted many of the same ideas found in Jesus's Gospels about the nature of emotional control, which is so important to all religious people. Since these religions and their founders lived in China and India several centuries before Jesus was born, we regard their ideas as antecedents to Jesus's teaching, which did not come into the world until at least five hundred years later. We must assume that Jesus was unaware of these prior ideas because of the great geographic and cultural distances involved.

The only conclusion we can draw from these parallels is that some of the ideas presented in Jesus's teachings were already out there in other parts of the world prior to Jesus's birth and ministry. It is not out of the question that God inspired men and women from other cultures to reach, by inspiration, the same ideas that Jesus presented to his time and culture five hundred years later. Here are some examples:

Jainism (India)

The warrior class in India during this time was very prideful, boastful, and violent. Their egotism, hatred, and greed fueled the warrior's ethos to become deeply entrenched within the warrior's heart. A warrior might declare, "I am the mightiest!" In contrast, the Jains attuned themselves to the pain and suffering of the world. They learned ways of meditation to expunge their hearts of these selfish, boastful emotions and instead focused their hearts on kindness and compassion. They were nonviolent and would kill no creature large or small.

Buddhism (India)

The focus for Buddhists was the equality of all people under the right ways of living. Meditation taught Buddhists that pain and suffering result from our attachments. Letting go of our attachments to our own selfishness leads us down the road to enlightenment. Be kind and compassionate to all. Never hate or hurt anyone. Live a life entirely free from all hatred and enmity!

Confucianism (China)

Confucius was an often out of work itinerant civil servant who worked, when he could find work, for various princes in the Han China of his day. In his *Analects*, Confucius taught the importance of the golden rule: "Do not do to others what you would not have them do to you." He used this as the basis of his system for social governance, which became the core for civil servant education in China for well over one thousand years. Confucius always taught that doing good was the highest purpose of any leader, and the systems he set up were based on exactly this principle. A true sage looked into his own heart to discover what it is that inflicts pain, and then he avoids doing this to anyone else.

Taoism (China)

Many early Chinese sages were careful observers of nature. For these sages, it seemed that all of the world, both in nature and within people's lives, revolved around constantly changing polar opposites that characterize our lives. Hot turns into cold. Light becomes dark. High becomes low. Rich becomes poor. The dance of the changing opposites is going on everywhere and always. However, in the middle of this storm of change, there is an eye of total calm and stillness called the Tao (Like I Am, not its real name). Meditations on the Tao teach us calmness and the importance of stepping out of the rushing cascade of change that is happening all around us.

Chapter 10

Jesus as the Light of the World

We now turn to see what God himself has to say about emotional duality. There is no better place to read God's statements on emotion than in the four Canonical Gospels of Jesus. Jesus lived from about AD 1 to AD 35. His public ministry was confined to the last two years of his life. Jesus taught that he had come to establish the kingdom of God on earth. Jesus first called disciples who would carry on the work of establishing the kingdom of God after he was gone from the earth. This work continues today.

During his time on earth, Jesus traveled around with his disciples, teaching and preaching to all he met. In our time, Jesus and his disciples and the women who took care of them would appear to be a band of wandering homeless people. He often talked to whomever would listen, healed the sick and the lame, and engaged in difficult discussions with many of the so-called legal experts (i.e. Scribes and Pharisees).

Jesus's teachings were in the form of words and works. His words were recorded by his friends in the four books we call the Canonical Gospels. His works were also recorded in the same four books. His works came in four forms:

- healing those who suffer from a number of serious medical conditions (blindness, crippling, leprosy, hemorrhaging, withered hands)
- driving out evil spirits (exorcism)
- controlling nature (control of gravity as evidenced by walking on water, multiplying material food items such as fish and bread, turning water into wine, raising the dead)
- forgiving sins

Jesus's works often seemed to serve the dual purpose of mercifully helping a suffering human being and identifying Jesus as the one sent by God, who is identical to God, because only God himself could accomplish the works done by Jesus.

Jesus's works can often be viewed as symbolic as in the case of curing blindness as a way of helping those who live in darkness come into the light. Exorcism is the way of banishing a negative spirit that is troubling an individual. Exorcism can also be thought of as turning one's selfish emotions into their virtuous duals. Saint Francis of Assisi so beautifully captured this emotional duality of selfishness turning into virtue more than seven hundred years ago in his famous prayer:

> God make me an instrument of your peace:
> Where there is hatred, let me sow love;
> Where there is injury, pardon;
> Where there is error, truth;
> Where there is doubt, faith;
> Where there is darkness, light;
> And where there is sadness, joy.
> O Divine Creator,
> Grant that I may not so much seek,
> To be consoled, as to console;
> To be understood, as to understand;
> To be loved as to love;
> For it is in giving that we receive;
> It is in pardoning that we are pardoned;
> And it is in dying that we are born to eternal life. Amen.

Jesus assured us in his Gospel words that he had come not to judge us but to save us. Save us from what? The best, and perhaps only, answer to this question is "from ourselves" in the form of following addictions to our own selfish emotions.

As our Savior, Jesus is always there to comfort us and help us reach out for him and accept his willingness to help us turn over the emotional coins within our hearts and transform the self-inflicted darkness within our hearts into the light of God's virtues. Following Saint Francis's beautiful prayer, we too can look carefully at Jesus's words within the four Canonical Gospels and find instances where Jesus is telling his listeners to turn internal selfishness into God's virtue at every possible opportunity.

The process of turning our selfishness into God's virtue can be thought of as a kind of emotional exorcism. Selfishness and virtue represent the two sides of the same dualistic coin. By turning over the emotional coin, we change our intentions of responding to the temptations of our own selfish desires into an acceptance of God's virtuous truths, which he grants to us by his grace.

The prayer of exorcism in *A Little Book of Meditations* is first and foremost intended to help free another person from emotional bondage. It was rewritten to serve as a guide for freeing ourselves from the bondage of emotional compulsions:

> This is a prayer for conditional power. This prayer is a very strong prayer; it is a prayer to gain control over myself. It is not in conflict with natural law in any way. This prayer is very ancient.
>
> O, Highest Most High, grant first upon me the strength and the power to use all my talents only for the highest of all causes. Now I ask of you the strength and the indulgence to transport my will around the heart and soul of your child that I may once again from elements stronger than myself, including even the negative aspects of myself, bestow upon me and instill within my heart those elements that will be used to compassionately control my emotional will when I struggle to make these decisions by myself. Lord Most High, I pray that I follow that which I pray is my better judgment in matters of emotional transformation. Lord of all, God Most High, bestow upon me the strength I need to do only that which is right in accordance with natural law to inspire upon my soul and ask for your total control in this matter. Lord of all, watch over me, thy servant, that I may have the courage to follow always the ways of truth. Amen.

This prayer is invaluable as long as it is used for the right and the good. It will serve you well.

The next four chapters contain instances from the four canonical Gospels where Jesus is calling us to let him help us turn over our emotional coins and partake of God's virtues by God's healing grace. Jesus's four Gospels are the prescriptions for helping us become full citizens in the kingdom of God as we change how we conduct ourselves emotionally once we have seen the light of his kingdom. To be successful in turning over the coin, we must pray and meditate on our ultimate goal of emotional transformation. This process can only be accomplished by way of God's grace, which is available to us through prayer, meditations, and dreams. Let us now turn to what each of the four Gospels teaches us about emotional transformation.

I have chosen to use an online red-letter Bible (King James Version) to be my Biblical reference for all four Canonical Gospels. Red-letter Bibles are Bibles in which all of Jesus's own words are printed in red ink. The reason for referring to a red-letter Bible is to ensure that every word spoken by Jesus will be considered as a part of my commentary on the emotional content in Jesus's words in each of the four Gospels, leaving no Gospel stone unturned. I recommend to all reader of this book that you choose a version of the Bible that suits you best and follow along by first reading each Gospel reference from your own Bible and then reading my commentary on the emotional content of that Gospel verse, which I have provided within the next four chapters.

The reader will notice a lot of similarities between the Gospel accounts of Matthew, Mark, and Luke. This is thought to be the result of a lost Gospel, called Q, which served as the source material for the first three Canonical Gospels. The Gospel account by John was written much later (about 90 CE) and is from a different source.

We assume that all four Canonical Gospels were based on eyewitness accounts that bear witness to the fine journalistic skills of their authors. Please follow along in the Bible version of your own choice as I describe how Jesus was speaking to us about the challenge of clearing our hearts of the darkness of our selfish emotions by asking for God's grace to turn over our emotional coins and reflect the bright light of the new emotions contained in God's virtues.

About half of this book is a commentary on how we, living in a scientific age, two thousand years later, can view and understand the emotional content of Jesus's words within the four Gospels. Within each commentary, the occurrence of an emotion within Jesus's words is noted, discussed, and explained in ways consistent with our twenty-first-century scientific thinking and ideas.

Reading the four Canonical Gospels is a rare opportunity that few Christians take advantage of. I urge you to do this for yourself! It is truly an amazing pilgrimage that you can take in your own home. Always remember that if the very heart of Christianity is anywhere, it is in the four Canonical Gospels. Read them, question them, digest them, and make them your own. As you read the following Gospel commentaries, I hope and pray that you get a lot out of it. However, it is far more powerful to read the Gospels for yourself, create your own commentary, and file it deep within your heart.

CHAPTER 11

Commentaries on the Emotional Content of Jesus's Words within the Gospel According to Matthew (follow along by first reading each verse in your own Bible before reading the commentary)

Matthew 4:10. Within Jesus's Gospels, the figure of Satan, or the devil, is often used as a personification of all that tempts us to act in selfish, emotional ways.

Matthew 4:19. Jesus calls us all to put down our nets and fish instead in the search for the lost souls of men and women in emotional torment.

Matthew 5:3. The poor in spirit are the humble. If we are to seek Jesus's kingdom of God, we must first accept by his grace the turning over of our selfish pride into the virtue of humility.

Matthew 5:4. To mourn is to be in the emotional state of sadness. Jesus will comfort those who are sad by turning, by his grace, their sadness into the virtue of joy.

Matthew 5:5. Like the poor in spirit, the meek are humble. Within the kingdom of God, once the prideful have been transformed by grace into the humble, they become the keepers of our earth.

Matthew 5:6. Those of us who reach out to receive Jesus's transforming grace will have our selfishness turned into righteous virtue.

Matthew 5:7. Once our selfish hardheartedness has been transformed by grace into the virtue of mercy, we can expect to receive God's mercy.

Matthew 5:8. Since we believe that no one can see God, this is a confusing statement. The heart, as used in the Gospels, indicates our emotional center. Perhaps as our emotional center becomes more and more virtuous by means of the transformations by grace, we are granted a clearer view of the reality of God. Or perhaps Jesus is saying it is by the purity of the emotions within our hearts that we perceive the presence of God within us. Or perhaps both are true at the same time.

Matthew 5:9. Peacemaking is a virtue. Consider Dr. Martin Luther King Jr. Jesus was a peacemaker, and Jesus was also a child (the Son) of God. Like Jesus, those of us who become peacemakers are regarded by God as his emotional children.

Matthew 5:10–11. A person of virtue is likely to be criticized and persecuted by selfish people who attempt to raise themselves up in the eyes of others by pushing others (those of virtue) down. Those who have achieved virtue are always welcomed into God's kingdom.

Matthew 5:12. The children of God have always been subject to persecution by selfish people. Walking God's path may not make you very popular with your selfish fellows but you have won God's favor by accepting, by his grace, the truth of God's virtues.

Matthew 5:13. Hold on to virtue (i.e. the savor of salt). Once it is lost, you have very little to fall back on.

Matthew 5:14. Those who lead lives of virtue will set an example for others by the success of their lives.

Matthew 5:15. If you are leading a life of virtue, you must show it to the world so all can see its advantages. People who speak the truth always draw attention to themselves.

Matthew 5:16. If you are a doer of good works, people will say that God is behind your good works.

Matthew 5:21–22. It is not only the doing of the acts themselves, but the holding on to the selfish emotions (within our hearts) that causes us to act selfishly, bringing judgment upon us.

Matthew 5:23–24. Settling an emotional dispute with another is a far greater gift to God than offering a sacrifice at the altar.

Matthew 5:25. Emotional disagreements need to be settled quickly before they get out of hand and the suffering is multiplied.

Matthew 5:27–28. If a man emotionally lusts after a woman in his heart, he has already committed adultery and rape in his heart, which tempts him to translate this emotion into a reality. The selfishness in the man's heart is the internal pollution that is blocking his own concentration from achieving virtue. This is the difference between the law and Jesus's teachings; the law deals exclusively with judging actions and works, while Jesus's teachings deal with the emotions that are stored within our hearts.

Matthew 5:29. Whenever a selfish emotion is threatening you, you must remove it by praying for God's grace before your entire emotional body becomes endangered by this emotional pollution.

Matthew 5:34–37. Refrain from swearing by anybody or anything. A simple yes or no is all that is required. To do more is to dive deeper into selfish emotional misunderstandings.

Matthew 5:38–42. If a man compels you to walk a mile, he has stolen your time and energy from you, making you resentful, which is selfish. If you choose to walk three miles instead of one mile, you have gifted him with your time and energy, which is the virtue of freely giving and generosity. An example of this practice is the Native American potlatch tradition.

Matthew 5:43–48. The point of these verses is the importance of the virtue of love above all else—and the danger of losing the love in your heart by hating another. We are all called by God to love our neighbors no matter what they do to us. They too have lives to lead and choices to make, and they too are God's children. They are struggling with themselves just as you are struggling with yourself. God loves all of us, which means we too are called to be like God and love all of God's children.

Matthew 6:16 and Matthew 6:2–6. In these verses, we are warned about doing good and kindly works as a public show where the real intent is to selfishly increase our sense of personal pride before others. Jesus says always give humbly with no big, self-aggrandizing fuss.

Matthew 6:7–8. When you pray, be brief. God already knows what your needs are. Don't repeat yourself for God already knows what you need, but he wants you to ask him for it.

Matthew 6:14–15. Forgive and forget truly in your heart. Don't hold a grudge after saying, "I forgive you." Remember that those who forgive will be forgiven.

Matthew 6:19–21. Nothing material is lasting. Material treasures all decay over time. The true treasures achieved in life are the spiritual treasures of learning to transform your selfish emotions into virtue by asking God, by his grace, to share his virtues with you.

Matthew 6:22–23. Strive always to fill your heart with the light. Never let the darkness enter your heart.

Matthew 6:24. No one can be selfish and virtuous at the same time. You are always called to make a choice. Making choices is the hardest and most important part of the human condition.

Matthew 6:26. Nature provides food for all members of the animal kingdom, including you. Why do you work so hard? Is all that effort really necessary? Do we waste time and energy on unnecessary work when we could be meditating on the emotional condition of what is in our hearts?

Matthew 6:28–30 and Matthew 6:33. You must work hard to provide fine clothes for yourself and your family. Is all this labor really necessary? Look at the beautiful clothes God has provided for the lilies of the field. God in nature provides so much for us without requiring enormous effort on our part. Rather, spend your time developing the inner emotional changes necessary to enter the kingdom of God, and God will add all else.

Matthew 6:34. None of us can predict the future. Don't even try. Deal with the challenges of today; it is enough.

Matthew 7:2. Don't be judgmental of your neighbors; you don't really know what is going on in their lives. It is selfish to judge. Your judgments will come back to you in both this world and the next.

Matthew 7:3–5. It seems to be our nature as human beings to see the faults in others far more clearly than we see the faults in ourselves. We need to heed the advice to first and foremost improve the state our own emotional lives, and refrain from offering criticism to others.

Matthew 7:6. Only share those things that are precious and holy for you with others who will appreciate them. Recognize that there are people who will scoff and make fun of that which is holy to you.

Matthew 7:7–12. Whatever you ask for earnestly in your heart will be granted; whatever you seek inside of yourself, you will find. The golden rule—do to others as you would have them do to you—neatly sums up all of the law and the prophets.

Matthew 7:16–19 and Matthew 7:24–27. Other people recognize who we are by our works. Those who do good works are known by them, but those who do bad works are known thusly. The wise build their lives on the firm foundation of virtue, but the foolish build their lives on selfishness. The foolish will find themselves slip sliding away in turbulent times, but the wise will be secure within their foundation of virtue.

Matthew 8:11. People everywhere, from every land, will hear Jesus's words and recognize their importance.

Matthew 9:2 and Matthew 9:12–13. Jesus describes himself as a physician who has come to heal those on the wrong path (sinners) and not those who are already righteous and filled with virtue.

Matthew 10:20. When you speak out of virtue, you are speaking out of the Spirit of God the Father. God the Father created virtue, and he has taught you to replace your selfishness with God's own virtue.

Matthew 10:21–22 and Matthew 10:34–39. These eight verses are hard to hear, but they carry elements of truth. The teachings of Jesus may divide families. Although today we call Jesus the "Prince of peace," Jesus did not promise us a peaceful life if we follow his teaching. We can expect push back, and utter rejection by the world, which is inherently selfish. In this world, all value is measured in money.

Matthew 10:40–42. Those who follow Jesus's teachings will carry Jesus to others. Those who do good works by following Jesus's teachings will be rewarded.

Matthew 11:27. It is Jesus who brings God the Father to us with his teachings.

Matthew 11:28–30. Jesus is promising his followers a life of humility and rest.

Matthew 12:11–12. Working on the Sabbath may be unlawful, but there is a higher law that says doing the good associated with a virtue is of the highest concern in all cases, seven days a week.

Matthew 12:25–26. Satan represents the temptations we all feel urging us to indulge in our own selfish emotions. Jesus is saying that if Satan's kingdom was truly divided, then our source of temptation has ceased, which is not very likely.

Matthew 12:28. Those who have found the emotional resources to ask Jesus for help have already entered the kingdom of God.

Matthew 12:29. By first defeating the strong emotional temptations within our own hearts, we have invited virtue to enter our hearts. To enter God's kingdom, we must first bring our own selfish emotions under control, so virtue can enter in.

Matthew 12:30. Those who are unable to hear and focus on Jesus's teachings are emotionally scattered in all directions.

Matthew 12:31–32. The Holy Ghost is the presence of God within our hearts. If we blaspheme against the presence of God within our hearts, we have condemned ourselves, which is hard to undo.

Matthew 12:35. Those who act in accordance with God's virtues in their hearts will do good works, and those who act in accordance with following the temptations of their own selfish emotions shall perform evil works.

Matthew 12:36–37. The things we say have meaning because they are the emotional description of what is in our hearts. At some point in the future, we will be required to give an account of how we have lived, and our words will serve as evidence. Think very carefully before speaking for no matter who you say it to, once the words are out, your words have acquired a life of their own and will come back to you someday.

Matthew 12:43–45. If a man or a woman has silenced the temptation of selfishness within his/her heart, but later allowed the selfish temptations to return, he/she will be worse off than before because the temptations will have multiplied.

Matthew 13:3–9 and Matthew 13:22–23. Those who continue to hold virtue in their hearts will do good works and be fruitful. Those who are turned away from Jesus's teachings by the selfish emotional temptations of the human condition will only do works based on our own personal selfishness.

Matthew 13:24–32. Like the mustard seed, the emotional virtues that God has planted in our hearts seem so small at first, but if allowed to flourish, they will bring forth a harvest of wonderful works.

Matthew 13:33. Leaven grows and spreads within all it touches. The teachings of Jesus also spread as people see the works of men and women who have heard Jesus's teachings and have put them into practice by asking God to replace the selfishness in their hearts with God's own virtues.

Matthew 13:36–39. The good seed is the teachings of Jesus. The man is any man. The enemy is the temptation of the selfish emotions. The tares are the bad works resulting from following our own selfish emotions, and the wheat is the fruit of following the emotions of virtue. Growing until the harvest is the man's lifetime, and memories of the selfish works in the man's lifetime will be destroyed, but his good works will become part of the eternal kingdom of God. If all the man does with his life is follow his own selfish emotions, there won't be much left of him in the end to become part of the kingdom of God.

Matthew 13:43–51. These additional parables describe the winnowing process by which the God-given virtues that we accept into our hearts will go on to become our part in the kingdom of God, but the selfishness of our hearts will be destroyed in the end. Since selfishness is a material thing (part of our DNA), it will not survive physical death.

Matthew 13:52. The treasured things both new and old are the emotions of virtue, which are brought to us by God. These include, but are not limited to, love, faith, trust, compassion, caring, empathy, forgiveness, courage, and generosity.

Matthew 13:57. It is a sad but true fact that we often get the least respect from the people closest to home.

Matthew 14:24–31. These verses tell the story of Jesus controlling nature (gravity) by walking on water. The disciples are at first afraid of the storm and are next overwhelmed with Jesus's control of nature. Peter controls his fears, and he alone asks Jesus if he too can walk on water. Jesus invites him to walk out on the water toward him. But halfway to Jesus, Peter begins to fear, raising doubts within him, and he starts to sink into the water. Jesus saves him with an outstretched hand. Jesus admonishes Peter for his lack of faith. The emotional lesson is that fear can destroy faith if we let it happen. Conversely, faith will banish fear if we can hold on to it. Through faith, Jesus is always there waiting to help us.

Matthew 14:33. By walking on water and controlling nature thusly, Jesus convinced the disciples of his true identity.

Matthew 15:11 and Matthew 15:17–20. Jesus is instructing his disciples that although many foods are unlawful, and handwashing before eating is required by the law, what is much more important is to keep your heart free of selfish emotions like evil thoughts of murder, adultery, fornication, theft, false witness, and blasphemy. It is the verbal expression of these selfish emotions that really defiles a person and not minor legal infractions.

Matthew 15:22–28. The Canaanite women pleads with Jesus to save her daughter from a devil who vexes her. Jesus tells her that he has been sent to save only the lost sheep of Israel, implying she is not included. The disciples consider her a pest and want Jesus to send her away. The woman, who is desperate, has great faith that Jesus can heal her daughter and argues her case with him (even the dogs under the table eat the crumbs left by the children). Jesus is moved by his compassion for her and her demonstration of a great faith in him and decides to heal her daughter.

Matthew 15:32. Jesus expresses his compassion (one of the greatest of the emotional virtue) for the multitudes.

Matthew 16:26–27. If someone were to own all of the earth's material treasures, his ownership would be only for a few short years (as long as his physical life lasted). Would this short-term ownership of material treasures be worth the sacrifice of his soul (i.e. the presence of God within the man's heart)? But the work that he does by way of the virtues in his heart will be his reward forever.

Matthew 17:20. If you have faith, one of the greatest of virtues, nothing will be impossible for you to do.

Matthew 18:3–6; Matthew 18:10; and Matthew 19:13–14. Children are very important to Jesus. Perhaps it is their combined virtues of wonder and humility in the world that sets them apart for Jesus's special praise. In another verse, Jesus tells us to be like little children if we are to enter the kingdom of God. The twin virtues of wonder and humility are essential if we are to enter the kingdom of God. Jesus states that harming a child is the greatest of all wrongdoing.

Matthew 18:8–9. These two verses are very difficult to understand. From the start, it is not clear what Jesus means by "offend." A best guess is that Jesus's admonition is that we work diligently to rid our hearts of the selfish emotions that may dwell there and replace them, through prayer by faith, with virtues.

Matthew 18:11. Jesus tells us once again that he has come to save us but not to judge us.

Matthew 18:15–17. There will always be times when disputes will arise between individuals. Resolving disputes is essential for both the good of the individuals and the good of the community. Try to resolve the problem first with the other individual, and if necessary, seek the help of the community. If all else fails, heed the words of a well-known Beatles song: "Let It Be."

Matthew 18:21–22. The virtue of forgiveness needs to be exercised as often as is necessary to bring about healing.

Matthew 18:23–35. If we are to expect unlimited forgiveness in the kingdom of God, we must always exercise the virtue of forgiveness with our fellows.

Matthew 19:17–26. With God, nothing is impossible. We are all saved by God's grace. The rich have their own special challenges.

Matthew 19:27–30. Many shall enter the kingdom of God, but their ordering will not be like in the world where the first shall be first and the last shall be last. In God's kingdom, the first shall be last and the last shall be first. Ordering in the kingdom will depend on virtues acquired and good works committed—and not on any kind of material wealth or power.

Matthew 20:2–16. God calls each of us for God's own reasons. We should not be seeking our own glory within God's call; we should be seeking to serve God in the ways we and God have agreed upon.

Matthew 20:25–28; Matthew 21:16; and Matthew 21:21–22. Jesus is naming faith as the most important virtue. If you have faith, then nothing you truly ask God for is beyond reach—even the control of nature. In the kingdom, you will be led by the humblest and those with the wonderment of a child.

Matthew 21:28–32. We must assume that Jesus is talking with a group of Pharisees and scribes. This is a very confusing verse because it would seem that Jesus is saying the second son had done the father's will more truly than the first, although the second son only gave his father lip service and not real service.

Matthew 22:36–40. Love in all its forms is the greatest commandment. We love our neighbor best by applying the golden rule to every situation.

Matthew 23:11–12. Humility is the key to opening the door to the kingdom of God.

Matthew 23:13–14. Hypocrites publicly play the role of sincere holy men while robbing widows and orphans in secret.

Matthew 23:15–19 and Matthew 23:24. In the case of the scribes and the Pharisees, there is nothing but selfishness. These people are addicted to their own self-interests.

Matthew 23:25. They pretend to have goodness on the outside, but they have nothing except self-interest on the inside.

Matthew 23:26–29. The Pharisees may look fine to others from the outside, but inside, they are a stinking mass of pride, greed, lies, lust, fear, and hatred. They are nothing but wolves in sheep's clothing.

Matthew 23:37; Matthew 24:6–10; 24:24; 24:29; 24:43; and Matthew 24:48; 24:49. Terrible things will always happen, and there is nothing we can do about it. The hour of their coming is unknown, but it is best to be prepared for the inevitable coming times of sadness and sorrow by looking into our own hearts to be certain they are filled with virtue instead of selfishness.

Matthew 25:2–13. We must all be emotionally prepared for the time and place of God entering our lives. There is no time to be wasted. We are being instructed (warned) to clean up the emotional household within our hearts as soon as possible. There is no time to lose because none of us know God's timing. We always need to be prepared.

Matthew 25:14–29. Put your God-given talents to work—or they will be taken away from you! These are words to live by.

Matthew 25:30. Our God-given talents and treasures are ours to use for increasing good in this world. God is counting on us to fruitfully invest the gifts he has given us.

Matthew 25:34–46. God counts on all of us to deliver kindness, compassion, empathy, and caring to all people who are in desperate need. When we deliver these virtues to the least among us, it is as if we delivered them directly to God himself. For God equates himself with the lowest and neediest members of humanity.

Matthew 26:6–12. The ointment was the woman's gift to Jesus, which she freely and lovingly gave. Clearly the woman loves Jesus dearly—with truly unbounded love and devotion. Putting the ointment on his head was her way of expressing her loving devotion to Jesus. This is a very beautiful story.

Matthew 26:26–29. Jesus enacts for the first time the sacrifice and sacrament of Communion. He lovingly gives himself to save all who come to him.

Matthew 26:37–41. The agony in the garden means that Jesus's time had now come. He prays that he will not have to go through this trial, but if it is God's will, he is willing to endure it. The spirit (that which is God) is willing, but the flesh (the selfish emotions of our physical DNA encoding) is weak. The emotion of this episode reminds me of an old country song: "You've got to walk that lonesome valley, you've got to walk it by yourself, nobody here to walk it for you, you've got to walk it by yourself."

Matthew 26:42 and Matthew 26:52. Jesus tells the disciples to put away their swords since he that lives by the sword will die the same way. One of Jesus's final acts on earth was to take a strong stand against violence and warfare.

Matthew 26:53–54; Matthew 27:46; and Matthew 28:10. Jesus is obedient to the last. In spite of death, he promises to see his disciples again in Galilee very soon.

Chapter 12

Commentaries on the Emotional Content of Jesus's Words within the Gospel According to Mark (follow along by first reading each verse in your own Bible before reading the commentary)

Mark 2:2. Jesus greets those sick of palsy with forgiveness after witnessing their faith.

Mark 2:8. Jesus was able to perceive the reasoning of others within his spirit. He knew what they were thinking and feeling.

Mark 2:9. Jesus asks them if it is easier to forgive sins or heal those sick with palsy?

Mark 2:10. Jesus healed this man so that the man and all others who witnessed this healing would know that he has a power that only can come directly from God.

Mark 2:17. Jesus is telling us that he came to heal the sick and not the well. Jesus is a physician treating the human emotions that work within our hearts.

Mark 2:22. New approaches require new thinking and new explanations that are required for acceptance.

Mark 2:25–27. Doing good (acting out God's virtues) is always more important than obeying the letter of the law.

Mark 3:4. Doing good (acting based on virtue) is more important than doing anything else on the Sabbath—even obeying the letter of the law.

Mark 3:5. Jesus is shocked by the hardness of heart shown by the witnesses (Pharisees?). Out of compassion for the man, Jesus healed his hand.

Mark 3:23–26. If evil were divided against itself, it would put an end to the existence of evil (Satan).

Mark 3:27–28. All our sins will be forgiven, including blasphemy, but the selfish emotions must first be eliminated from your heart.

Mark 3:29. The Holy Ghost is the God within each of us. If we disrespect the God within us, we disrespect ourselves—and there is little hope for our future.

Mark 3:30 and Mark 3:33–35. Jesus considers all believers to be his true family members.

Mark 4:3–9. Those who hear Jesus's teachings and really internalize them are like a fruitful tree that passes seeds along to many other locations. A single believer can pass along Jesus's teachings to many other people. However, many other people will also hear Jesus's teachings and ignore them because of their greed and lust.

Mark 4:10–19. A man whose heart is filled with the selfish emotions of greed and lust will not hear Jesus's teachings and become unfruitful. Temptations to do selfish acts overwhelm this man and make him unfruitful.

Mark 4:30. Those who internalize Jesus's teachings are those who become fruitful by spreading Jesus's teachings to others.

Mark 4:21. The shining light of Jesus's teachings should not be hidden away; they must be put on display so all can learn from it.

Mark 4:22. All secrets will become known, including those contained in Jesus's teaching.

Mark 4:23–4:24. Be open to Jesus's teachings because more will be shared.

Mark 4:25–29. Those who fruitfully share Jesus's teachings pass the teachings on to others who are to be numbered among those who will be saved at the harvest.

Mark 4:30–32. The virtues contained within Jesus's teachings will grow into something very large as the kingdom of God, in spite of its humble beginnings. The kingdom of God is built on the person-to-person spreading of Jesus's teachings.

Mark 4:38–39. Jesus has the ability to control nature, but only God can control nature.

Mark 4:40. Jesus is shocked by their lack of faith.

Mark 4:41. The disciples now knew for certain that Jesus had to come from God since even nature obeyed him.

Mark 5:6–8. In our times, we liken the unclean spirit to the temptations and compulsions within a person to obey their own selfish emotions.

Mark 5:9. Selfish emotions come in many different forms, and they sometimes work together. For instance, fear, frustration, anger, and hate may all team up to form an unholy alliance within a person.

Mark 5:10–13. This exorcism makes sense because the pig is unclean according to the law, meaning the unclean spirits would find a familiar home in the uncleanliness of the pigs.

Mark 5:14–15. Such an exorcism was beyond these people's understanding, and it filled them with great fear.

Mark 5:16 and Mark 5:19. Jesus was filled with compassion for this man.

Mark 5:30. Jesus senses within his heart that the spiritual power of his virtues had gone out to someone he had touched.

Mark 5:31–33. The woman, sensing that she had been healed by the grace of Jesus's virtue went and fell down before him. Even touching Jesus carries his healing power.

Mark 5:34. Jesus attributes her healing to her faith in him. Jesus had not only healed her physical condition, but because her constant blood flow was unclean, according to the law, Jesus healed her place within Jewish society.

Mark 5:38–41. Yet another case of Jesus controlling nature by bringing the dead back to life.

Mark 5:42–43 and Mark 6:4. Jesus's experiences were of not being taken seriously by his own family, friends, and neighbors.

Mark 6:5. Their disbelief made it difficult for Jesus to perform his healing works.

Mark 6:6–7. Jesus is training the twelve disciples to continue his work of building the kingdom of God with healings and exorcisms after he is gone.

Mark 6:8–9. Perhaps Jesus foretold that the people the twelve would meet on their journey would feel less threatened and more compassionate toward them if they came dressed in utter simplicity. Jesus had directed his disciples to lead lives of total humility.

Mark 6:10–11. These are the rules of the road given by Jesus to his missionary disciples. Jesus is looking forward and seeing how acceptance of his teaching will be vital to the ultimate survival of these communities.

Mark 6:12. To repent means to ask that the selfishness of their hearts be changed, by God's healing grace, into virtue.

Mark 6:13. The missionaries were granted many of the same powers (preaching, repentance, exorcism, and healing) that Jesus had during his human existence.

Mark 6:34. Jesus was moved with compassion for the people who were as sheep without a shepherd. Jesus taught them how to live in the kingdom of God.

Mark 6:40–43. The food was multiplied as an act by Jesus of controlling nature.

Mark 6:49. Their fear made it difficult for them to recognize that it was Jesus walking on the water.

Mark 6:50. Jesus calms their fears by reassuring them that it is indeed he who walked on the water, an act of controlling nature.

Mark 6:51. The disciples were gripped in equal measure of fear, wonder, and amazement.

Mark 6:52. They could not believe their eyes because it was impossible for their heads to accept what Jesus had just done. With God, everything is possible, but the disciples needed to find other, more acceptable explanations for what had just happened.

Mark 7:5–6. The prophets before Jesus had experienced hypocrites who gave lip service to God but did not honor God in their hearts (their hearts were filled with selfishness and not virtue).

Mark 7:7. These people insist on following the commandments of men (selfishness) and not the commandments of God (virtues).

Mark 7:8. For these people, it had become more important to wash pots and cups than to hold love, compassion, and kindness within their hearts.

Mark 7:9. When it becomes inconvenient for men to love others and be compassionate and kind to others, they turn to their own traditions of selfishness.

Mark 7:10–13. Using the selfish traditions of man as a way of avoiding God's call to adopt his virtues as replacements for our own human selfishness, is a big mistake.

Mark 7:14–23. People are defiled not by what they eat, but by the verbal expressions of the selfish contents of their hearts. Jesus will save us if we ask him, by God's grace, that our selfish emotions be flipped into godly virtues. If we ask him, God will help us change the hate within our hearts into love. We must ask God by prayer and meditation to enable us, by his grace, to make these changes.

Mark 7:25–29. Because of the woman's faith in him, and her persistence, Jesus is moved by compassion to heal the daughter of the tormenting temptations within her heart, even though she is not a member of the people Jesus was sent to save.

Mark 8:2–3. Jesus controls nature by multiplying the loaves and fishes out of his compassion and caring for these fasting people.

Mark 8:11–12. Jesus must be deeply frustrated with these people who refused to take his teaching seriously and keep demanding some kind of sign (material proof) of who he is. It seems that so many people, then and now, demand black-and-white proof of something that can only be understood within our hearts. How do you prove the reality of God? Of course you can't, but you can experience it within your own heart.

Mark 8:15. Jesus tells his followers to beware of the Pharisees and all they stand for.

Mark 8:16–17. Be patient. The truth will be revealed in time, and if your hearts have not been hardened, you will experience the truth.

Mark 8:18–21. Jesus is speaking to the hardhearted and saying, "How many times do I need to offer you proof of who I am?"

Mark 8:31–33. Peter was understandably shocked to hear Jesus predicting his own execution. Peter was looking at the situation from a human perspective, and although Peter clearly wanted nothing to happen to his hero, Jesus's execution might have been a part of God's plan. To not consider that Jesus's execution might be a part of God's plan, Peter was thinking and speaking out of his own selfish human wishes. No one should ever tell God his business.

Mark 8:34–35. If we save our lives by profiting from our own selfishness, what spiritual value have we added to our lives? If we are able to put aside our selfishness, eliminate our hearts' selfishness, and accept virtue, by the grace of God, we have saved our life spiritually.

Mark 8:36. If we gain the whole world by our selfish living, what is our profit? Nothing at all of spiritual value has been achieved.

Mark 8:37. What is the dollars and cents value of virtue?

Mark 9:23. Those with real faith can achieve their most treasured personal goals.

Mark 9:24. The father of the stricken child cries out with tears in his eyes for God to please help him with his unbelief. At some point, we all need to cry out to God to help us with accepting virtue as the replacement for our selfishness.

Mark 9:25–34. The dispute over who will be the greatest is caused by selfish pride and is counter to the virtue of humility.

Mark 9:35. A desire to be the first in a selfish human way sends you to the back of the line in the kingdom of God.

Mark 9:36–37. The wonder and innocence of a child is of very great value to Jesus and in the kingdom of God.

Mark 9:38–40. He who is not against us is for us. If a man can perform an exorcism in Jesus's name, he is surely for us.

Mark 9:41. If a man does a kindness for you in Jesus's name, his reward in the kingdom is secure.

Mark 9:42. Above all, the sacredness and vulnerability of all innocence children is of the highest importance.

Mark 9:43–45. The selfish emotions within your heart can poison the emotions within your heart, and they must be removed (transformed) by prayer and meditation. If they remain unresolved, the selfish emotions in your heart will lead you down the road to hell.

Mark 9:47–50 and Mark 10:2–12. Jesus is upholding a woman's right as a co-human being to be part of any decision-making concerning a marriage.

Mark 10:13–14. Jesus is teaching the disciples that it is the wonder and innocence of little children that is most highly prized within the kingdom of God.

Mark 10:15. Those who will enter the kingdom of God will enter it as little children, filled with wonder, innocence, and humility.

Mark 10:16–18. All good (virtue) comes from God. Since God is good, good (i.e. virtue) is from God and is God.

Mark 10:19. These are the approved and disapproved works from the law.

Mark 10:20–21. Jesus loved the man and knew that for this man to become spiritually complete, he needed to fill his virtue cup with generosity, kindness, compassion, and humility. Filling one's virtue cup is much harder to do than simply obeying the letter of the law.

Mark 10:22. This rich man was clearly facing some difficult emotional choices.

Mark 10:23. The possessions of a rich man enslave him to selfishly guard his material wealth rather than acquiring the spiritual riches of virtue.

Mark 10:24. The ultimate selfishness is to trust in our own material riches.

Mark 10:25. The rich find it very difficult to trust in God. They fall prey to thinking their salvation lies in their own bank accounts.

Mark 10:26–27. Anyone who truly wants to be saved and enter God's kingdom will enter because God will find a way. God is truly "Infinite Possibility."

Mark 10:28–30. Those who follow Jesus's teachings will be rewarded and enter the kingdom of God.

Mark 10:31. The rich and the famous will enter the kingdom of God last, and the humble will enter first.

Mark 10:32 and Mark 10:34. Jesus is predicting the unfoldment of his own destiny.

Mark 10:37–40. The ordering of those within the kingdom of God will be God's choice alone.

Mark 10:41–45. Humility and servanthood are the chief factors in determining who is first within the kingdom.

Mark 11:15–17. Jesus is filled with righteous indignation over how God's house is being misused by those trying to steal money from the people.

Mark 11:23–24. Whatever you ask God for in prayer, you must truly believe that you will receive your request—for it is to happen.

Mark 11:25. First, forgive those who have mistreated you before you pray to God to forgive you. To be forgiven, you must first forgive others.

Mark 11:26–33. Jesus knew that it would be impossible for them to answer the question he gave them. In this way, Jesus defused one of the tricks used by the scribes and the Pharisees to trick him into saying something they could use to arrest him.

Mark 12:2–9. The servants are the prophets, Jesus is the heir (who will be killed), and the husbandmen are all people.

Mark 12:10. Jesus is being rejected by his own people, but his teachings will be spread far and wide. Jesus will become the head cornerstone everywhere.

Mark 12:14–17. Jesus left the decision up to those who asked the question, but since Caesar's image is on the coin, the implication seems to be that all wealth is ultimately Caesar's, but that which is spirit is God's.

Mark 12:24–27. After bodily death, people will assume new lives, like angels, in heaven.

Mark 12:29–31. This is the great commandment that in all ways love is number one in our lives. Jesus commands us to love God in every possible way and to love our neighbors (all other human beings) in the same way we love ourselves. Never do to another person what you wouldn't want done to you. The golden rule is universal and is followed by people of all religions everywhere.

Mark 12:33. Love is greater than all the burned sacrifices that can be imagined. It is our love that joins us to God.

Mark 12:34. After Jesus's love command, everyone there was in shock and could think of nothing else to ask or say.

Mark 12:38–40. The scribes pretend to be holy men, but they had no love in their hearts. Rather, they enjoyed puffing up their pride by wearing fancy clothes and receiving salutations in the marketplace. If they had a chance, they would rob widows and orphans.

Mark 12:41–43. The poor widow has given all that she has out of her love for God. She has literally thrown herself on God to take care of her because she now has nothing material to fall back on. Jesus remarks that the widow's gift, which is all she had, is worth far more than all the money in the treasury because she gave everything she had out of her love for God. Her real gift was not the coins but her love of God.

Mark 12:44 and Mark 13:5–6. Be aware—there will be many pretenders following me.

Mark 13:7–8. There always will be trouble happening in earthly life. There is much to sorrow over.

Mark 13:9 and Mark 13:11. In your hour of trial, God, the Holy Ghost, will always grant you the right words to say. Fear not.

Mark 13:12–13. The world is a dangerous place, and there are no assurances of what the future may hold. Always trust in God to get you through the worst the world has to offer.

Mark 13:14; 13:23–25, 13:29–31. No matter what happens in the future, the teaching of Jesus is always with us. If you follow it, you will be saved.

Mark 13:34–35. Although we need be watchful, no one knows when Jesus will return. However, his teachings will always stand. No matter what happens, we must follow what he has taught us.

Mark 13:37 and Mark 13:3–14:7. What this woman did for Jesus was an act of absolute surrender in the form of her pure, sweet, adoring love for Jesus.

Mark 14:22–25. Jesus shares a final meal with his friends who he will meet again in the heavenly kingdom of God.

Mark 14:29–31. Peter is impulsive. Jesus knows that Peter's brave vow to always be there for him is sincere but not likely to be carried out due to his temptations by fear.

Mark 14:34. Even Jesus needs a friend at this terrible time.

Mark 14:35–36. Jesus prays that he may be spared what he must endure, but he promises to follow God's will—no matter what happens.

Mark 14:37. Jesus is disappointed to find his friend Peter asleep.

Mark 14:38. Prayer will guard you against the temptations of the weak flesh (selfish emotions), but we pray for the virtues within our hearts to remain strong.

Mark 14:48–49. Jesus is shocked that so many of the men who have come to take him with swords, as they would a common thief, are the same men who he taught at the temple.

Mark 14:50. This must refer to the disciples.

Mark 14:51–52. The identity of the young naked man remains a mystery. Perhaps the linen cloth is intended to be Jesus wrapped in death.

Mark 14:55–62. Jesus answers the high priest directly and tells him who he really is.

Mark 14:63–64. The high priest is so angry that he wants to kill Jesus on the spot because Jesus is claiming to be God.

Mark 15:2 and Mark 15:34. Jesus dies feeling in a state of total abandonment by both his friends and by God.

Mark 16:5–6 and Mark 16:9. Jesus's first appearance on Easter Sunday was to Mary Magdalene, who has loved him dearly.

Mark 16:10–11. The disciples did not believe Mary Magdalene. Perhaps it was more than they could hope for or expect. They must have forgotten about how many others Jesus had raised from the dead. Why not himself?

Mark 16:12. Perhaps Jesus was in the process of making the slow transition from his human form into a purely spiritual form as the Son of God.

Mark 16:13–14. Jesus is amazed by their lack of faith and belief.

Mark 16:15. Jesus trusts the same disciples to go out into the world and preach the Gospel in every place, to every creature.

Mark 16:16. Those who believe will be saved, and those who do not believe will not be saved.

Mark 16:17–18. Jesus predicts that his followers will have the power to rid others of their selfish temptations, quickly acquire the new languages of new lands, and heal their sick.

Chapter 13

Commentaries on the Emotional Content within the Gospel According to Luke (follow along by first reading each verse in your own Bible before reading the commentary)

Luke 2:46–50. This story is a first sign that Jesus's understanding of scripture was something more than human.

Luke 4:1. We assume Jesus was led by the Spirit of God.

Luke 4:2. We think of the devil as the personification of the selfish emotions that *tempt* us into doing things that are counter to the virtues of God's plan for us.

Luke 4:3–4. Jesus refuses to accept any command from the devil. This is an example for all of us to follow.

Luke 4:5–7. The devil is offering Jesus all the wealth, riches, and power on earth. To accept the devil's offer, Jesus must agree to serve temptation (personified by the devil) by indulging in all of the selfish human emotions such as anger, hate, fear, greed, lust, and pride etc.

Luke 4:8. Jesus refuses to serve Satan (the combined temptation to indulge in all the selfish human emotions) and states that he will serve only God. This is good advice for us all to follow.

Luke 4:9–12. Jesus states, "Never tempt God." This is a kind of ultimatum to our selfish human ways.

Luke 4:13–14. When Jesus returned to Galilee, he was filled with the Spirit of God. His fame was spreading.

Luke 4:17–21. The prophet Esaias is filled with the Spirit of God and has been commanded to preach the Gospel to the poor, heal the brokenhearted, preach deliverance to captives, return sight to the blind, and set the bruised to liberty. Jesus announces that he is the fulfillment of this prophecy.

Luke 4:22. The crowd is amazed and wonders who Jesus *really* is.

Luke 4:23–27. How could Jesus possibly know all these details unless he were speaking directly from God.

Luke 4:28–29. The crowd intended to kill him for blasphemy because he spoke a truth that they were unable or unwilling to accept.

Luke 4:30. Jesus escaped death by the grace of God.

Luke 4:30. The spirit of an unclean devil is the selfish emotion that has taken control of this man. As an example, consider a man so "out of control with anger" that no one can even talk to him about his problems.

Luke 4:34. It is our badly out-of-control, selfish emotions that first recognize our own need for God.

Luke 4:35. As Jesus performs the exorcism, the man is thrown to the ground, but when he gets up, he is healed of his controlling emotion.

Luke 4:36. The people wonder about the source of Jesus's authority and power.

Luke 4:43. Jesus tells the people that he has been sent to preach the establishment of the kingdom of God to all people in all places.

Luke 5:9. This is another example of Jesus's control of nature, which could only come from God.

Luke 5:10. Jesus says to James, Simon, and John, "Don't be afraid. I need your help in establishing the kingdom of God."

Luke 5:11. James, Simon, and John accept the call from Jesus. They left their old lives behind to work with Jesus to establish the kingdom of God on earth.

Luke 5:12–14. Jesus has cured the man of leprosy, but he wants him to go to the priest to be officially declared healed and whole because leprosy was understood to be an "uncleanness" under the Law of Moses in those times.

Luke 5:19–20. Jesus forgives the man's sins, which is understood by many to only be the domain of God. The man's faith that Jesus can cure him is the inspiration for his cure.

Luke 5:21–25. Reading their internal thoughts, Jesus is saying to the conniving scribes and Pharisees that he can forgive sins and heal a seriously ill man. Only God or one sent from God can do these things.

Luke 5:26. The scribes and Pharisees were thrown into a state of shock by what they saw.

Luke 5:27–28. Levi follows Jesus at his call.

Luke 5:31–32. Jesus states that it is his mission to help those who are emotionally lost to seek repentance by turning their selfish emotions around and following God's virtues. Those who are already leading lives of virtue do not need Jesus's help.

Luke 5:36–39. Those who are undergoing the emotional conversion of changing the selfish emotions in their hearts into the virtues of God must avoid every vestige of their old lives in the same way someone who is being healed of alcoholism must stay out of barrooms. For example, new wine must never be put into old bottles.

Luke 6:2–5. Jesus, as God's messenger, is himself the Sabbath.

Luke 6:7–11. It is driving the scribes and Pharisees crazy because Jesus refuses to fall into one of their traps. It doesn't seem to occur to them that they are standing in the presence of God, and they don't even recognize it. Perhaps, in their hearts, they are atheists. For them, it is easier to keep the letter of the law than to let virtues like faith enter their hearts.

Luke 6:18–19. Jesus provided healing to those possessed by unclean spirits and out-of-control, selfish emotions by sharing of his virtue with them. Healing always comes about by accepting God's virtues as the replacements for the selfish emotions that are vexing us.

Luke 6:20. The humble poor will enter the kingdom of God straightaway.

Luke 6:21. By accepting God's help, we will be emotionally fed by God's virtues, and our sadness will be transformed into God's joy.

Luke 6:22. Those who are convinced that the way of the world (selfishness) is the only way to live will hate those who follow the path of virtue and consider them to be demented. If you become a follower of virtue, the world will reject you and consider you a pariah in the same way the scribes and Pharisees rejected Jesus.

Luke 6:23. Even if the world rejects you, heaven will not.

Luke 6:24. Being rich is its own reward, but it counts for nothing in the kingdom of God. You can't buy your way into heaven.

Luke 6:25. As the song says, "Riding high in April, shot down in May."

Luke 6:26. It may feel good to have other people speak well of you, but what you really should be seeking is God's virtues within your heart.

Luke 6:27–28. This command is hard to hear, but it is important. Our enemies are also God's children, and God loves them too. Hard as it is, we must love and do good things for our enemies who, like ourselves, are also God's children.

Luke 6:29. The emotional point here is that if a man requires you to do something you don't want to do (hit you on the cheek, require that you walk an extra mile, etc.), and you do only the bare minimum required of you, you will hate the man because he has taken from you something that is yours. However if you go the extra mile, above what is required, you will be giving the man a gift and will feel loving and charitable (virtues) toward him. The Native Americans recognize this principle in their potlatch tradition.

Luke 6:30–6:31. The golden rule can be found throughout history. Confucius based his entire legal/organizational system upon the golden rule.

Luke 6:32–35. To follow virtue is to always do what is good in all cases. To count up your profits before doing good is to serve greed and not virtue.

Luke 6:36–37. How can we expect God to be merciful and nonjudgmental with us if we don't do the same for others?

Luke 6:38. This is an excellent way to think about karma. If we give out love and care, we will ultimately receive back love and care. However, if we give out hate and anger, we will ultimately receive back hate and anger. This rule is a fine example of emotional conservation.

Luke 6:39. Since the blind cannot lead the blind, if you wish to learn about virtue, you must follow someone who is virtuous. A selfish person cannot teach you to be virtuous.

Luke 6:40. To seek instruction, you must seek out someone who is already a master at their trade.

Luke 6:41. It is so much easier to see the failings of another than to see our own failings. If we are to learn and improve, we must concentrate on realistically evaluating our own failings. Another person's failings are his or her own business. Criticism is a selfish emotion, but acceptance is a virtue.

Luke 6:42. Only help another person with their emotional problems after you have solved your own emotional problems. Otherwise, you will be the blind leading the blind.

Luke 6:43. A virtue-filled person cannot produce selfishness. A selfish person cannot produce virtue.

Luke 6:44. If we are seeking virtue, we must look for it in virtuous men and women. If we are seeking selfish emotions, we must look for them in selfish men and women. Virtue does not produce selfishness. Selfishness does not produce virtue.

Luke 6:45. The emotional abundance within one's heart determines the path taken with one's decisions. Virtuous people speak words of virtue. Selfish people speak word of selfishness.

Luke 6:46. As creatures of free will, we follow our own hearts as we make decisions.

Luke 6:47–48. God is the rock of our foundation. God grants us, by grace, his virtues to follow, which enables us to make good emotional decisions.

Luke 6:49. Those who do not live on a foundation of God's virtues only have their own selfishness to depend on in times of stress, which will let them down every time.

Luke 7:8–9. Jesus recognizes that faith is where you find it—and it can be with anyone and with all people.

Luke 7:10–15. Jesus raised this man from the dead out of the compassion he felt for the man's widowed mother.

Luke 7:16. People were beginning to recognize who Jesus really is.

Luke 7:19–21. Many healings occurred at this time.

Luke 7:22–35. John is criticized for not being a social person who eats bread and drinks wine with the social elite. People say that John has a devil. Jesus is criticized for being a social person who eats and drinks wine with the social elite, and he is called a glutton and a winebibber. You just can't win in the world of public opinion.

Luke 7:37–48. Jesus forgives the woman's sins and is touched by her faith and love, which are solely focused on him. The woman's great love for Jesus is very touching to him, for in it, he sees love, the greatest of all virtues, being brought to full flower.

Luke 7:49–50. As Jesus said in many other places in the Gospels, he came not to judge us but to save us. God's forgiveness is the most important part of our being saved. For we are our own biggest enemy, in particular when our overwhelmingly selfish emotions run amuck.

Luke 8:2–3. Many very special women followed Jesus and his disciples as they roamed around preaching, teaching, exorcising, and healing. At least some of these women, like Mary Magdalene, had been healed by Jesus in exorcisms. It is not clear if any of these women were also Jesus's disciples. I wonder if any of the women wrote down what would be their Gospel accounts based on their days of traveling around with Jesus. It would be fascinating to hear their firsthand account of Jesus healing them of their many emotional scars.

Luke 8:4–10. Many people will not understand the explanation that the disciples received. For these people, parables are the best route to understanding.

Luke 8:11. Jesus is teaching.

Luke 8:12. Temptation leads these people away from Jesus's teaching.

Luke 8:13. These are the people who hear the teaching, but because they have no firm foundation, they will forget about the teaching and be tempted later into selfish behavior.

Luke 8:14. Cares, riches, and pleasures of the world will push these people off the emotional path of virtue straight into their own selfish emotions.

Luke 8:15. Those who hear and cherish the teaching will live lives of virtue and goodness. In this way, they will bring forth fruit for all to see.

Luke 8:16. Once you know the teaching, share it with others. Your life will be a light to lighten the way for others.

Luke 8:17. Sooner or later, every secret becomes known.

Luke 8:18. Listen very carefully to the teachings to ensure that you have gotten them right.

Luke 8:21. Jesus's family is all those who hear and follow his teachings.

Luke 8:22–24. The disciples are filled with fear of the storm. Jesus calms the raging waters and they are saved.

Luke 8:25. Jesus questions them about what happened to their faith. The disciples wonder who Jesus is and how he is able to control the forces of nature.

Luke 8:30. Jesus cured this man of his legion of temptations.

Luke 8:39. The cured man told everyone about how Jesus cured him.

Luke 8:45–46. Jesus perceived that a woman had touched him—and virtue had gone out of him and into the woman.

Luke 8:48. Jesus assures the woman that because of her faith in him, she has been cured of her medical symptoms.

Luke 8:49–50. Jesus tells the man to have faith, and his daughter will surely come back to life.

Luke 8:51–53. The weepers and doubters did not believe that Jesus could bring the girl back to life.

Luke 8:54. Jesus made the weepers and the doubters leave and asked the girl to get up, which she did as her spirit came back into her body.

Luke 8:55–56. Jesus charged the parents not to tell anyone what had happened.

Luke 9:2–4. Jesus sent the disciples forth to teach and heal all who would hear. He told them to stay and eat with whoever invites them as long as they remain in that city. Jesus tells them to be humble and take only one coat each.

Luke 9:5. If a city will not receive you, shake the dust off of your feet as a testimony of being unaccepted in that city.

Luke 9:14. Very large crowds were gathering to hear Jesus speak. His fame is spreading fast.

Luke 9:20. Peter understands who Jesus really is.

Luke 9:22. Jesus knows which way the wind is blowing and predicts his own fate.

Luke 9:23. Following Jesus involves self-denial (or perhaps denying his own selfish emotions) and suffering.

Luke 9:24. Letting go of a comfortable material life may be the price that must be paid for finding one's spiritual life.

Luke 9:25. If you gain the whole world materially and lose your life spiritually, what have you gained?

Luke 9:26 and Luke 9:38–43. Jesus healed the son of seizures, which sound like epilepsy.

Luke 9:46–48. Jesus once again affirms the holiness of children. The least of whom are childlike in their sense of wonder, amazement, and innocence, and will be among the greatest in the kingdom of God.

Luke 9:49–50. Those who are not against us are for us. Why stop someone who is doing good—even if he is a stranger?

Luke 9:52–56. Jesus has not come to destroy anyone but to save all who are in need of salvation.

Luke 9:58. Clearly Jesus feels homeless and rejected. He may be suffering from being on the hard road of a homeless teacher and healer.

Luke 9:59–9:60. Spreading the kingdom of God may require letting go of some of the rules and practices of men on certain occasions.

Luke 9:61–62. Jesus is telling this man that he needs to make a serious commitment to spreading the kingdom of God.

Luke 10:1. Spreading the kingdom of God is now becoming a major effort. The new advanced troops would first make known to the townspeople that Jesus is coming before he actually gets there.

Luke 10:2–9. More workers are needed to spread the good news of the kingdom of God. The workers are told to only stay in one house with one family while they are preaching and healing in a given city.

Luke 10:10–16. In the end, it will not go well for places who reject Jesus.

Luke 10:18–19. The workers have gained the power to successfully cast out the temptations of the enemy.

Luke 10:20. Your joy should not be in having power over evil spirits (selfish temptations) but in the knowledge that you are welcome in heaven.

Luke 10:21–22. We will learn about God in a childlike way that is taught to all of us by Jesus.

Luke 10:23–24. Jesus is telling his disciples to recognize how really special their experience of God in Jesus really is—and to be sure they value it that way.

Luke 10:25–37. Jesus is telling us that it is not the letter of the law—the man was covered in blood, which would have made the priest and the Levite ritually unclean—that counts, but our willingness to express God's virtues in practicing kindness, compassion, and caring for the injured man. Even though the helping man is a foreigner, and despised by the community, it is this man who shows the injured man caring, compassion, and empathy and is his true neighbor. This does not mean the law is wrong, but acting on the emotions contained within God's virtues adds a whole new dimension of understanding to this story.

Luke 10:38–42. Mary has chosen this particular moment to talk with Jesus and express her love for him. She has chosen to ignore all of the "must dos" and "got to dos" that her sister is fretting over.

Luke 11:1–2. Jesus is praying for the establishment of God's kingdom.

Luke 11:3. We hope.

Luke 11:4. We pray for and practice forgiveness and ask for God's help to avoid temptation and all the evil it creates.

Luke 11:5–10. Pray to God to help you find a way to do those things that you can't see how to do ourselves. Have faith that God will be there—and answer your prayer no matter what it may be for.

Luke 11:11–13. God knows what you need. Have faith in God and ask him for what you need.

Luke 11:15–19. Do you want to be judged by someone who is in a league with the devil?

Luke 11:20. But by casting out devils (temptation) with the finger of God, the kingdom is being steadily built. More men are strong, and fewer men are tempted by the devil.

Luke 11:21–23. This verse seems in direct contradiction with the "he that is not against me is for me" verse. I think the contradiction is resolved by realizing that we need some team players on our side if we are to build the kingdom. Simply being not against me does not make someone a team player; it simply means the other is not actively trying to destroy the kingdom.

Luke 11:24–26. When exorcising a serious temptation, be vigilant not to let down your guard and let back in the original temptation, which may bring along some of his comrades in arms, who will be even more difficult to exorcise. If pride was the original temptation—and if pride brought hate and fear—how much more difficult it would become to put an end to all three of these temptations?

Luke 11:29–33. Word about Jesus and his works is bound to get around far and near. People everywhere will sit up and take notice when they see the light of God shining through Jesus and his teachings.

Luke 11:34–36. Beware of the darkness in your heart; it can choke out the light of God's virtues shining within you.

Luke 11:38–54. The scribes, the Pharisees, and the lawyers try to trick Jesus into saying something that they can accuse him of. Jesus says, "Isn't the existence of love in our hearts far more important than all the details of the law and all the prideful acts carried out by the Pharisees, scribes, and the lawyers?"

Luke 12:1–5. Beware those who threaten to poison your heart with the temptations of pride, greed, and prestige.

Luke 12:6–7. God knows and counts all parts of us and our world down to the smallest detail. God greatly values human beings and will do all he can to protect and support us.

Luke 12:8. If you praise God to other men, you will be blessed by the angels of God.

Luke 12:9–10. Blaspheming against the Holy Spirit is the same thing as saying there is no God within us. Such a statement is hard for God to forgive because it is so condemning of the one who said it because it suggests there is nothing godly within the one who said it.

Luke 12:11–12. God the Holy Spirit will always be there for you in your hour of need.

Luke 12:13 and Luke 12:15. Covetousness is a serious selfish emotional problem that many people suffer from. Native American people have successfully treated this problem by participating in a giveaway ceremony called the potlatch.

Luke 12:16–21. Material wealth will do nothing to help your spiritual health. You can't buy your way into heaven!

Luke 12:22–31. The real work of our lives is not to build wealth but to build God's kingdom.

Luke 12:32–34. Where your treasure is, your heart will be there also. If your treasure is in a bank your heart will be there too. If your treasure is with the virtues of God, your heart will be there too.

Luke 12:35–40. Be prepared—none of us know how much time we have. When we are granted an opportunity to build the kingdom, don't waste it.

Luke 12:41–48. More domains to administer come with more responsibility and more expectations.

Luke 12:49–59 and Luke 13:6–16. It is better to do good by helping others who are suffering than to follow the letter of the law and miss the chance of doing good. All of us are encouraged to do good whenever we can. Try not to let little details get in the way of doing good.

Luke 13:17. Many people were getting the point of what Jesus was saying: God's healing is of far greater importance than the letter of the law. "Was the Sabbath created for man or was man created for the Sabbath?"

Luke 13:18–21. The kingdom is like, in all examples, a growing thing that carries itself into everything it comes in contact with.

Luke 13:22–30. Jesus is telling us that there is no sure ticket of admission to the kingdom of God. And the entry may be the reverse of what people are expecting: the first shall be last, and the last shall be first. Conventional wisdom is probably of no help. Even keeping every letter of the law is certainly no guarantee of admission.

Luke 13:31–34. Jesus knows that he is heading up to Jerusalem to die.

Luke 13:35 and Luke 14:7–11. Humility is an extremely important virtue.

Luke 14:12–14. Be kind and helpful to those who have a hard time in life. Even a little kindness means so much to them.

Luke 14:15–24. Never turn down an invitation from God. It may not be repeated, and others may accept the same invitation in your stead.

Luke 14:25–33. To be Jesus's disciple, you must cut all ties with the everyday world and live only for God and not for the concerns of men.

Luke 14:34–35. If your purpose in life has been lost, it may be difficult to reclaim it.

Luke 15:2–7. Because the weights and measures of God are so different from those of man, it is very difficult for men to understand leaving behind the ninety-nine sheep and going off in search of the one lost sheep.

Luke 15:8–10. Each one of our spiritual advancements is of immeasurable value to God.

Luke 15:11–20. The father is filled with compassion and caring for his son. The father forgives him, kisses him, hugs him, and takes him home.

Luke 15:21–24. The father holds a big party to celebrate the return of his son because he is overcome with joy and gratitude that his lost son has returned home to him.

Luke 15:25–28. The oldest son was angry and jealous because he had always been the devoted son and never received a party like the one his brother received.

Luke 15:29–32. The father is celebrating the return of his wayward son, who, as in "Amazing Grace," once was lost but now is found, was blind but now he sees.

Luke 16:1–11. To be trusted by God to be faithful with spiritual riches, you must first be faithful in all your dealings in the material world with the people of that world, including bankers, lawyers, and businesspeople.

Luke 16:12–13. Serving two masters inevitably leads to hatred and anger and must be avoided if at all possible.

Luke 16:14–15. The values of man are not the values of God.

Luke 16:16. The domain of the law ended with the coming of the kingdom of God.

Luke 16:17. There is nothing wrong with the law. It is perfect, but its time has ended on account of the coming of the kingdom of God.

Luke 16:18–26. The first shall be last, and the last shall be first. Once mortal life has ended, the opportunity for behavioral change has come to an end. Make wise choices while you can.

Luke 16:27–31. If they can't follow Moses and the prophets, then no one can reach you.

Luke 17:1–2. Children are very special to Jesus. He is very concerned about the possibility that any child could be harmed.

Luke 17:3–4. Forgive, forgive, forgive—as many times as it is necessary.

Luke 17:6–9. Always thank your servants whenever they help you and be kind and respectful toward them.

Luke 17:10–19. Only the Samaritan returned to thank Jesus for his healing; the other nine just took off. How ungrateful they were.

Luke 17:20–21. The kingdom of God is not in an external place; it is found deep within our hearts.

Luke 17:24–37 and Luke 17:1–2. Pride and humility are different sides of the same emotional coin. What God is looking for is for us, with God's help, to turn over the coin and change our selfish prideful nature into a heart and soul of deep humility.

Luke 18:15–17. Jesus tells us that we must have the wonder, surprise, and innocence of a small child if we are to enter the kingdom of God.

Luke 18:24–25. Riches and wealth are a terrible burden for those who would enter the kingdom of God. Where your wealth is, that is where your heart is.

Luke 18:29–33. Jesus predicts his own death again.

Luke 18:34–42. By faith, the man is healed of blindness.

Luke 18:43 and Luke 10:8–17. Success in small areas leads to trust in larger areas.

Luke 19:18–24. The money from the man who did not make a profit was transferred to the man who made a large profit. Trust results from successfully following orders and using your own creativity to gain profit.

Luke 19:25–27 and Luke 20:4–17. The chief priests are fearful that the parable is about them, and they fear the people will follow Jesus and throw them out of the temple. Perhaps other people will be received into the kingdom of God.

Luke 20:23–36. The children of God will become like angels.

Luke 20:37–38. God is the source of all life.

Luke 20:46–47. The crafty scribes convince everyone that they are holy men while they devour widows' houses at the same time.

Luke 21:2–3. The widow's mite is of more value to God than all the donations of rich men. She gave her very all.

Luke 21:4. The widow has contributed her entire material life!

Luke 21:5–6. Nothing material last forever.

Luke 21:8. Beware of imposters.

Luke 21:9–15. Don't worry. The spirit will guide you when you are on the spot! Trust in God!

Luke 21:16–20. Historic fact: Jerusalem was destroyed after a long siege by the Romans in 90 AD.

Luke 21:21 and Luke 21:26. Fear will be everywhere and in everyone.

Luke 21:29–36. Be vigilant. A time of great change is coming. Don't be caught unaware.

Luke 22:16–20. Jesus shares his body and his blood with his friends in the form of bread and wine.

Luke 22:21–22. The betrayal is about to begin.

Luke 22:25–27. Jesus portrays himself as a humble servant of others.

Luke 22:28–29. Jesus passes the task of establishing the kingdom on to his disciples.

Luke 22:30. Perhaps Jesus is talking here about the heavenly kingdom of God. Perhaps the heavenly kingdom is an extension of the earthly kingdom—or could it be the other way around?

Luke 22:31. Jesus recognizes that Simon is being tempted by Satan, but Jesus is praying that Simon's faith will not fail him.

Luke 22:32–34. Remaining brave and strong in the face of temptation is very difficult. Peter will be challenged by his own fear.

Luke 22:40. Jesus tells us to diligently and prayerfully avoid the temptation of selfishness.

Luke 22:42. If this cup is your will, I will do it.

Luke 22:43. God sends Jesus an angel of strength and courage to help him. Angels are God's messengers.

Luke 22:44. Jesus is in agony trying to resist the temptation to avoid following God's will.

Luke 22:46. Don't sleep. It may only lead you into temptation.

Luke 22:52–53. Why do you come for me in the darkness of night—like I am a criminal?

Luke 22:67–70. Jesus knows they are plotting to destroy him.

Luke 22:34. They killed Jesus and cast lots to divide his clothes.

Luke 22:46. Jesus dies.

Luke 24:17–39. The resurrected Jesus still has a body.

Luke 24:41–43. Jesus ate food to demonstrate that he did have a human body. He was not yet fully returned to his spiritual self.

Luke 24:44. Jesus is no longer with the disciples, but he reminds them what the Law, the prophets, and the psalms said about him must be fulfilled.

Luke 24:45–48. Jesus tells his followers to go forth into the world, to tell his story, and preach repentance and forgiveness of their sins.

Luke 24:49–52. Jesus promised his followers that God would send them power.

CHAPTER 14

Commentaries on the Emotional Content within the Gospel According to John

(follow along by first reading each verse in your own Bible before reading the commentary)

John 1:1–5. The darkness does not understand the light of Christ.

John 1:17. The law is a written list of rules, all the do's and don'ts, but the teachings of Jesus concerns God's grace and truth.

John 1:18 and John 1:38–40. Jesus is God's only begotten Son. Andrew and Peter were followers of John the Baptist.

John 1:41. Andrew says to Simon Peter, "We have found the Christ."

John 1:41–43. Jesus invites Philip to follow him.

John 1:47. Jesus invited Nathanael (in whom there is no guile) to follow him.

John 2:3–10. Jesus controls nature as a way of convincing people that he has come from God because only God can control nature. The meaning of this story is very hard to understand (righteous indignation perhaps?). It is hard to picture an angry Jesus.

John 2:16–25. Most men are filled with selfishness.

John 3:1–3. Only with the wonder and innocence of a child is it possible to approach God.

John 3:4–8. All who are born of the Spirit hold virtue in their hearts.

John 3:9–15. If you believe in Jesus, eternal life will be yours.

John 3:16–17. God sent his son not to judge the world but to save the world from itself.

John 3:18–19. The darkness of selfishness is what many people love.

John 3:20. Evildoers cannot stand the light because their evil deeds will be exposed for all to see.

John 3:21. Those who follow the truth seek the light in that their deeds may shine as products of God.

John 4:7–10. Jesus is inviting the woman to ask him who he is and offers her the "living water."

John 4:13. Living water is that which quenches one's thirst forever, but you will always be thirsty in time after drinking water from a well.

John 4:14. The living water contains the virtue that is everlasting and springs upward to eternal life with God.

John 4:15 and John 4:20–24. God is Spirit and must be worshiped in the Spirit and in truth.

John 4:26. Jesus tells the woman that he is I Am.

John 4:38; John 4:44–45; and John 4:48. For many, belief depends on the proof of signs and wonders. Jesus accepts this situation as a fact.

John 4:49–50. The man had faith that Jesus had cured his child.

John 5:14. Jesus tells the man that he is forgiven (made whole) and to go forth and lead a life without sin.

John 5:22. Jesus says that the Father has delegated judgment to the Son (Jesus).

John 5:23. To honor the Son is to honor the Father. To not honor the Son is to not honor the Father.

John 5:26–27. Jesus has been given the authority to judge.

John 5:28. Even those who once lived will come to know Jesus.

John 5:29. Those who have lived before will be judged and sent on to their eternal destinations.

John 5:30–32. The witness of God is the real witness.

John 5:33–36. Jesus will bear witness to *all* virtue.

John 5:37–38. The people did not believe the prophets.

John 5:39–42. If you don't have the love of God in you, you will not receive Jesus.

John 5:43. People will receive only other humans and not spirits.

John 5:44. How is it that you can trust in other people, but you cannot trust in God?

John 5:45 and John 5:47. Moses wrote of Jesus, but people still do not believe in Moses's writings.

John 6:12. Jesus controls nature by multiplying the fragments of bread.

John 6:17–20. It is Jesus walking on the water, controlling the nature of gravity. Don't be afraid. Have faith in one who can do such things.

John 6:21 and John 6:27. Jesus offers us all the virtues, which leads to everlasting life.

John 6:28–29. The work is to do the work of God by believing in Jesus (by faith).

John 6:32–6:33. Jesus himself is the true bread of heaven to be shared by all of us. He offers us the truth and the love of God.

John 6:34–35. Jesus himself is the embodiment of all virtues!

John 6:38. Jesus came down from heaven to do God's will (spreading virtue) and not his own.

John 6:39. No one will be lost, but all will be raised up in virtue on the last day.

John 6:40. All who come to know Jesus will have their lives changed from selfishness to virtue, and they will have everlasting life.

John 6:44. God's tiny starbursts of virtue draw us to Jesus.

John 6:45–48. Jesus is the source of all the virtuous nutrition in our lives.

John 6:49–51. Jesus's living bread consists of the virtues he is teaching us.

John 6:53. The bread and the wine represent the virtues that Jesus embodies and is leading us to.

John 6:54–56. We dwell in Jesus, and he dwells in us. If we truly believe, then we all share in his virtues.

John 6:57. If you eat Jesus's body and drink Jesus's blood, you will be alive in him. This is the best way God can help us understand that we take Jesus into ourselves by eating his flesh and drinking his blood. It sounds grisly, but if we look beyond the obvious and see this statement in a very fundamental way to mean that we incorporate the virtues of Jesus into our hearts in the same way we incorporate food into our bodies. As the food we eat becomes a part of our physical bodies, the virtues Jesus teaches us will become part of our hearts.

John 6:58. Jesus invites us to eat his flesh and drink his blood as the living bread and the living water become a part of who we are and last forever. The living bread and the living water bring us the virtues that replace our inherent selfishness natures. We must eat the living bread and drink the living water by practicing prayer and meditation. This process of prayer and meditation is to be our lifelong pursuit.

John 6:60–63. Jesus's words are the Spirit and are truly our real life. The flesh accounts for nothing in time. Just as Jesus is in the Father and the Father is in Jesus, we are in Jesus, and Jesus—and Jesus's virtues—is in us.

John 6:64–71. Jesus always knew that Judas would betray him.

John 7:6–7. The world hates Jesus.

John 7:8. Jesus is fully human and fully divine.

John 7:16–17. To do God's will, you must know God's teaching of virtue.

John 7:18. If a man speaks for himself only, he seeks only his own glory.

John 7:22–23. If you can circumcise a man on the Sabbath, why can't you heal a man on the Sabbath?

John 7:24. Judge according to all virtue.

John 7:28. Jesus is sent by God.

John 7:29–38. Out of Jesus's will flow the living waters containing *all* virtue. If we accept them, we will be baptized in the virtues of the living waters.

John 8:6–12. Let he without sin cast the first stone. They all put down their stones and left because they felt guilty about their sins. The light is of *all* virtue.

John 8:14–19. This must have sounded like blasphemy to those who heard him in the temple.

John 8:20. His hour must include arrest and execution.

John 8:21. Because of their selfish emotional states, they cannot follow Jesus into God's kingdom.

John 8:14–19. "Of this world" means a state of emotional selfishness.

John 8:24. "Die in your sins" means held back spiritually because they lead entirely selfish emotional lives.

John 8:25. Jesus doesn't repeat himself.

John 8:26. Jesus speaks for God.

John 8:28. After his execution, men will know that Jesus really is sent from God.

John 8:29. God and Jesus are one, and Jesus does the will of God.

John 8:31. Hearing Jesus's words makes anyone Jesus's disciple.

John 8:32. We are set free of our emotional selfishness by the knowledge of the truth of all God given virtues.

John 8:34. If you allow yourself to be selfish in your heart, you have become a servant of your own selfishness and temptations.

John 8:35. Those who follow their own selfishness will not exist forever.

John 8:14. Jesus's words will set you free because the virtue they teach will replace your selfishness by the act of redemption through God's grace. The price to be paid is for God to accept and cancel the validity of your selfish emotions. Many Christians regard the pain of Jesus's death on the cross as the price God paid for redeeming our selfish emotions.

John 8:37–38. Jesus's father is God; a human being's father is also a human being.

John 8:39–40. Kill the messenger!

John 8:41–42. The people who Jesus is talking to really don't get it!

John 8:44. People who lie, cheat, steal, lust, and murder are following the will of their father, the tempter (the devil), who tempts people into acting out of their own selfish emotions.

John 8:45–58. Jesus declares that he is eternal.

John 8:59. The crowd tries to kill Jesus, but he escapes by going right through the crowd.

John 9:1–5. Since Jesus's words enlighten all who hear them, we say his words "shine like a lamp."

John 9:6–33. Jesus's identity, like all of us, is "proven" by his works.

John 9:34–41 and John 10:1–4. The sheep know his voice because they recognize that he speaks the truth.

John 10:5–7. Jesus's words lead the sheep in the right direction to the right door.

John 10:8. The sheep ignore the thieves and robbers.

John 10:9. Jesus is the shepherd who is the door to eternal life.

John 10:10. The thief only comes to steal and kill and destroy; Jesus comes to offer us an abundant life.

John 10:11. Jesus gives up his life on the cross to save the sheep. Jesus offers redemption to anyone who asks. His offer of redemption involves the transformation of our selfishness into virtue by God's loving grace. *All* virtues will follow.

John 10:12–15. Jesus is the Good Shepherd who lays down his life for the sheep. Jesus offers us, the sheep, redemption by changing our selfishness into virtues by God's grace.

John 10:16. Are these other folds other religions, other cultures, or other universes?

John 10:17–18. Jesus lays down his life as a gift freely given. In laying down his life, Jesus offers us the redemption of changing our selfishness into virtue. He loves us, and we love him, and he draws us to him by his transforming grace.

John 10:25. Jesus's identity is created by his teachings and his works.

John 10:26. Those who do not believe are not Jesus's sheep, and they do not follow him into redemption.

John 10:27–28. True believers are granted the gift of eternal life.

John 10:29. Once we are with the Father, we cannot be removed from the Father by any man.

John 10:30–10:31. The crowd tries to kill Jesus. They refuse to believe in him and think they must kill him.

John 10:33. Those who want to kill Jesus do not understand that Jesus can be both man and God at the same time. This is the holy duality of Jesus and the Father.

John 10:34–38. His works identify Jesus as being from God, including Jesus's control over nature. Jesus's most important work is redeeming us by transforming our selfishness into virtue by God's loving grace.

John 11:4. The sickness is our own selfishness, which Jesus has come to heal.

John 11:9. Those who walk in the light are not confused by darkness. These people do not stumble.

John 11:10. We stumble in the emotional darkness because we have no one to light our path. We depend on Jesus to light our path by redeeming our selfishness into virtue by the transformation of God's loving grace.

John 11:11. Jesus woke Lazarus out of the sleep of death and brought him back to a fuller, richer life of virtue.

John 11:14. Jesus raises Lazarus from the dead as one more work of identification that he was sent by God.

John 11:23. Jesus assures Martha that her brother will rise.

John 11:24–25. Jesus raised Lazarus both as proof that he is from God and as a demonstration of the resurrection that can be accomplished for all of us by the redemption of our selfishness into virtue.

John 11:26. It is Jesus alone who holds the key to eternal life for all of us.

John 11:34–35. Jesus is filled with sadness for the loss of his friend.

John 11:36. Jesus is filled with love for his friend Lazarus.

John 11:47–48. If Jesus is not killed, all the people will believe in him and in the kingdom of God, which means the Romans will destroy Israel and kill everyone because they will fear a revolution.

John 11:49. Caiaphas says that with some creative thinking, Jesus's success can be put to the useful purpose by saving Israel from destruction by the Romans.

John 11:50. Jesus is cast into the role of scapegoat who will save Israel from murder and destruction by the Romans. Caiaphas was not entirely wrong considering that Jesus's death on the cross was the work of his ultimate redemptive act.

John 11:51–52. Caiaphas prophesied that the believing Jews at home and the believing Jews all over the world would be saved from the terrors of Rome by Jesus's death as the scapegoat.

John 11:53. Planning Jesus's murder to save the people—or was it for their own selfish gains? This is a prime example of the ends justifying the means.

John 12:3. Mary, filled with the spirit of her love for Jesus, anoints Jesus's feet with very costly ointment and wipes his feet using her own hair as a towel. The sweet smell of the ointment is everywhere. It is a touching scene.

John 12:4–6. If the ointment were sold, Judas planned to steal the money.

John 12:7. Mary anointed Jesus's feet both in joy and in sadness because she must have known that he was soon to be murdered. This scene reminds me of how the civil rights advocates of sixty years ago all agreed they were willing to die for the cause because of its supreme importance to their people. Martin Luther King Jr. was the one who, like Jesus, paid the ultimate price to free his people.

John 12:8. Jesus advises his friends to celebrate his presence because he will not be with them much longer.

John 12:9. Raising Lazarus from the dead drew a lot of public attention.

John 12:10–11. Their friends feared for Jesus's life and for Lazarus's life—just as the friends of Martin Luther King Jr. did.

John 12:23–24. Once in the ground, the seed will change and bring forth a plant that will feed people.

John 12:25. Clinging to the selfish emotions of this life may endanger your hope for eternal life.

John 12:26. Serving Jesus by choosing virtue is serving God.

John 12:27. Jesus is troubled facing the hour of his death, but this work is what he came to do.

John 12:28–29. Everyone who was present heard something different.

John 12:30–31. The prince of this world, the temptation of selfishness (the devil) will be cast out by Jesus's redemptive acts.

John 12:32. As Jesus returns to heaven as a pure Spirit, all men who believe in him will be drawn up to follow Jesus into heaven.

John 12:35. Walk in the light as long as you can; or if the darkness comes, you may not know the way. Enjoy the presence of Jesus for as long as you can because he will be leaving soon.

John 12:36. Jesus hid himself from his friends. Why? For prayer and meditation?

John 12:44. Believing in Jesus is the same as believing in God.

John 12:45. He who sees me sees God. How can this be? Perhaps seeing Jesus is as close as any human being can come to seeing God.

John 12:46. Jesus and his virtues *are* the light of the world.

John 12:47. Jesus came to save us—not to judge us.

John 12:48. Those who reject Jesus's words will be judged on the last day.

John 12:49. Jesus speaks the words of God—for God.

John 12:50. God's commandment is life eternal for all of us.

John 13:7–14. In the way we serve God, we should also serve one another. The last shall be first, and the first shall be last. Jesus is the humblest servant of all.

John 13:15–16. Equality of the Servant and the Lord (Jesus and God).

John 13:17–20. Receiving Jesus is the same thing as receiving God.

John 13:21. The coming betrayal makes Jesus so sad.

John 13:26–27. Jesus said to Judas, "Now that Satan is in you, go do what you must do and be quick about it."

John 13:31. God and the Son together will now be glorified.

John 13:32–34. Jesus commands us to love him and love one another. To embrace the emotion of love is the newest and greatest of all commandments.

John 13:35. Discipleship is defined by and in our love for one another.

John 13:36. Not now, Peter, but later, you will follow me.

John 13:37. Jesus knows that Peter will deny him.

John 14:1. Believe always in both God and Jesus.

John 14:2. Jesus will make a place for us in heaven.

John 14:3. You will be with me wherever I am.

John 14:4–6. Jesus is the Way, the Truth, and the Life of God's virtues.

John 14:7–10. The Father is talking through Jesus because the Father is in Jesus and Jesus is in the Father. They are the both the same, but they are also each unique.

John 14:11. Believe in me because you have the faith that Jesus and the Father are one and/or because of Jesus's works.

John 14:12. You can also do similar works if you have faith.

John 14:13. By faith, ask what you will in Jesus's name—and it shall be done.

John 14:14. Just ask in my name—and it will be done.

John 14:15. Love Jesus by following his commandments and embracing God's virtues.

John 14:16. The Holy Spirit will be within you forever.

John 14:17. You will receive the Spirt of Truth and the Spirit of Truth shall be within you always.

John 14:18. Whenever we need him, Jesus will come to us to bring us comfort.

John 14:19. Jesus will live on, and by faith, we may see him whenever we need him.

John 14:20. Know there is a full circle of connection: Jesus is in the Father, you are in Jesus, and Jesus is in you.

John 14:21. Those who love Jesus will have Jesus inside of them just as Jesus has the Father inside of him. Both Jesus and the Father will love you, and you will love them both.

John 14:22–23. We love Jesus by keeping his words, and if we do, both Jesus and the Father will love us and live within us.

John 14:24–26. The Holy Spirit will be our teacher and our guide.

John 14:27. Don't be troubled and afraid. Accept the peace that Jesus brings to us, accept the courage from God to overcome our fears, and live as Jesus would have us live.

John 14:28. Rejoice because Jesus is going to the Father, and he will return to us later. The Father is greater than Jesus. I think our human reason fails us at this point.

John 14:29–30. The prince of this world, Satan, is the temptation of our own selfishness.

John 14:31. Go forward because Jesus is always with you.

John 15:1–2. The Father is the husbandman, Jesus is the vine, and we are the branches. Branches that do not bear fruit will be removed from the vine, but from those branches that are fruitful, the harvest will be gathered.

John 15:3. My words will clean your soul by bringing my virtues into your heart.

John 15:4. Jesus is the source of all virtue. Since Jesus and the Father are one, the source of virtue is God—and virtue is from God.

John 15:5. We think of living in virtue as bringing forth fruit. God is the Source, and we are the expression.

John 15:6. Those who do not abide in Jesus's virtues will be cast away from the vine and be destroyed.

John 15:7. God will grant the wishes of the virtuous—just ask.

John 15:8. The virtuous bear much fruit and become Jesus's disciples.

John 15:9. Love flows from God to Jesus and into all of us by the virtues that we keep within us and show to the world as we are required to.

John 15:10. We must keep Jesus's commandments of virtue just as Jesus keeps God's commandments and abides in God's love.

John 15:11. We experience joy when the virtues of Jesus fill our hearts.

John 15:12. Jesus's greatest commandment is that we love one another as he loves us.

John 15:13. The virtue of love is practiced most perfectly in laying down your life for your friend—as Jesus has done for all of us.

John 15:14. Those who follow Jesus's commandment to love one another are his friends.

John 15:15. A friend shares intimate truths about himself or herself with their friend.

John 15:16. Since Jesus has chosen each of us, we will bear fruit. Whatever we ask of God in Jesus's name will be granted.

John 15:17. The virtue of love is above all else.

John 15:18. The world hates you because the world is selfish and expects you to do the same, but you are not selfish.

John 15:19. You do not follow the emotions of selfishness, which are of the world, but you have turned them into the emotions of virtue by the grace of God.

John 15:20. Expect the world to treat you as the world has treated me.

John 15:21–22. Having heard Jesus's teaching, people cannot hide from their own misdeeds.

John 15:23. To hate Jesus is to hate the Father—the two cannot be separated.

John 15:24–25. There is no basis in the Law for their hatred of me. They have hated me out of their own selfishness.

John 15:26. The Father, Jesus, and the Spirit of Truth, who is the Comforter, are all in agreement and are all of a single origin.

John 15:27. Citizens of the kingdom of God will bear witness to who I am.

John 16:1–2. Men may kill you thinking they are doing God's work—consider all of the wars of religion over the centuries.

John 16:3. Those who do these things do not know either the Father or Jesus.

John 16:4–7. Jesus must go away to send us the Holy Spirit.

John 16:8–11. The prince of this world is the temptation of selfishness. The Holy Spirit will judge the temptations of selfishness to be unsound and temporary.

John 16:12–13. The Spirit of Truth is God as the God of truth.

John 16:14–15. The Spirit of Truth will show you all that is true.

John 16:16. Jesus goes to the Father in a little while.

John 16:19–20. Let your sorrows be turned, by Jesus, into joy.

John 16:21. Childbirth is an example of how our anguish can be turned into joy.

John 16:22. No man can take away your joy when you see Jesus again.

John 16:23–24. Ask in my name and you will receive what you asked for—and your joy will be ever overflowing.

John 16:25. Jesus promises to plainly show his friends the Father.

John 16:26–27. The Father loves you because you love me.

John 16:28 and John 16:31. Do you have faith?

John 16:32. Jesus predicts his friends will be scattered, but he will not be alone because God is with him.

John 16:33. Your peace and joy come from Jesus and his virtues, and your trouble comes from the world of temptation to selfishness.

John 17:1–2. Jesus asks God to grant eternal life to all his friends.

John 17:28 and John 17:31. Jesus's work on earth is now completed.

John 17:5. Jesus is asking the Father to return him to a purely spiritual state. Glorifying is the achievement of that purely spiritual state.

John 17:6. Jesus has shown God to his friends who were given to him by God.

John 17:7. Jesus's gifts of virtues are from God alone.

John 17:8. The gifts that Jesus has shared with his friends are his teachings.

John 17:9. Jesus prays for his disciples, who may one day be all of us.

John 17:10. Those who are mine are yours, and those who are yours are mine also. The Spirit of Jesus resides in them all.

John 17:11. Jesus asks the Father to unite all believers into a oneness like the oneness of Jesus and the Father. Many believers call this oneness the Body of Christ.

John 17:12. Among the disciples, only Judas was lost. All of Jesus's other friends are safe.

John 17:13. Jesus asks the Father to help believers find the virtue of joy in Jesus everywhere in their lives.

John 17:14. Believers are hated by the world because the world knows they are not the same as other men who are of this world.

John 17:15. Jesus asks the Father to protect believers from the evil temptations of the world.

John 17:16. Jesus believes his friends are not of this world—just as Jesus is not of this world.

John 17:17. Jesus asks the Father to bring all believers into the knowledge of the Spirit of Truth.

John 17:18. Jesus has sent the believers out on a mission to establish the kingdom of God in this world.

John 17:19. We will know the Truth, and the Truth will set us free.

John 17:20. Jesus prays for all believers who will become believers because Jesus's friends will spread the kingdom of God far and wide, around the world.

John 17:21. Jesus prays that all believers will remain one and bring about the founding of the kingdom of God.

John 17:22–23. Jesus tells us that the Father loves him in the same way Jesus loves all believers.

John 17:24. Love unites all of us to Jesus and to God and to one another.

John 17:25. Jesus is the link that joins the Father and the world. The virtues of the Father are passed on to us by Jesus.

John 17:26. The love of God, which is in Jesus, will also be in us.

John 18:8. Jesus asks the guards to let his friends go. I am who you seek.

John 18:11. Jesus wants no violence. What is about to happen is supposed to happen and must happen by the will of God.

John 18:20–23. Why punish me for doing and saying good?

John 18:34 and John 18:36. Jesus's kingdom is the spiritual kingdom of God, which resides within the hearts of all believers.

John 18:37. Jesus is a king bearing the Truth to his kingdom.

John 18:37. Was Pilate an idiot or a philosopher?

John 19:11. Jesus's fate was preordained.

John 19:26–16. Mary recognizes the risen Jesus, and her sorrow is instantly turned to joy. Jesus is in the process of turning from being human to being divine—quantum mechanics would say his particles are becoming waves again—and he cannot be touched by Mary at this moment.

John 20:18–19. The risen Jesus who walks through walls is becoming less human and more Spirit.

John 20:20. Jesus showed them his hands and his side so they could believe that he had indeed risen from the dead.

John 20:21. Fear not for you are about to start out on a great mission.

John 20:22. Jesus gives his disciples the Holy Ghost.

John 20:23. The disciples are granted the authority to forgive sins.

John 20:24 and John 20:26. Jesus came through the walls again to greet Thomas.

John 20:21–29. The great faith of those who have not seen but believe anyway is recognized.

John 20:30. Jesus then did other works that are not written down.

John 20:31. Thank you so much, John. You have produced a beautiful Gospel.

John 21:5–15. Jesus is asking Peter to become the husbandman to the flock.

John 21:16–17. Because Peter loves Jesus, Jesus trusts Peter to go out into the world and take care of the needs of the faithful.

John 21:18. In their old age, we must help others get around.

John 21:22. Perhaps Jesus wants Peter to stay in the world until he returns.

Chapter 15

Conclusion and Reflections

The teachings of Jesus were originally planted in the fertile soil of the eastern Mediterranean. Many early Christians were drawn to Jesus's teachings because they offered both realistic and satisfying alternatives to the Roman state religions of their time. However, by the fourth century, many Christians held important state jobs and had much influence with the leading politicians of their day. In the remarkable year of AD 321, Emperor Constantine declared Christianity to be the Roman Empire's state religion. Suddenly, Christians changed from being a despised minority to becoming the new political movers and shakers of their time.

Not all Christians were pleased with this development. Many saw danger on the horizon since Christians became politically powerful for the first time. Many even worried that political power might corrupt the new religion's mandate to spread Jesus's teachings and establish his kingdom of God on earth. These Christians had serious doubts about the possibility that the Roman Empire could ever truly become the kingdom of God.

"The last shall be first and the first shall be last, and the humble shall inherit the kingdom" seemed like an unlikely future for the powerful Roman Empire with all its military might. However, like it or not, the institutional church was born in AD 321. During the coming dark ages, when the power and influence of the empire was in decline, the emperor's role was gradually taken over by the bishop of Rome. The pope became simultaneously the head of the church and the head of the state. Since that time, in one way or another, in Europe, the state and the institutional church have become like Siamese twins joined at the hip for all time.

Many Christians of this time were not pleased with the joining of church and the empire. In Egypt, there was a movement of proto-monastics who renounced their material lives to seek out a bare existence of fasting, meditation, and prayer. Many of these "desert fathers and desert mothers" lived in caves along the Nile River. At one time, more than ten thousand people lived in this way.

The desert fathers and desert mothers depended on meager donations from friends and family to keep them from starving. Their activities were for the most part engaging in prayer and meditation while reading and reflecting on Bible verses. In this way, they felt they were doing their part for building the kingdom of God one little bit at a time, based on their humility and love for others.

In some cases, the desert fathers and mothers took their practice to extremes by sitting for days on top of tall poles or standing on one foot for many hours. In these cases, the desert fathers and desert mothers adopted practices that were remarkably similar to the Yogis of India. Their goal was to still the mind of all its selfish desires and concentrate on being open to the presence of God in the hope of receiving visions and signs. Some desert fathers and mothers were among the first Christians to recognize that demonic attacks and an individual's own out-of-control, selfish emotions, such as a man who is mad with anger, are truly one and the same.

More than a millennium later, in the land that was to become the United States, a young minister named Roger Williams reached a startling conclusion for his time and place. Williams lived in the Massachusetts Bay Colony along the Atlantic coast of North America. During this period, the church in Massachusetts Bay was controlled by a sect of the Anglican Church called the Puritans. The Puritans also controlled all of the political affairs of Massachusetts, making Massachusetts truly a theocracy where church and state had become one. Williams, as a Christian minister, thought this was all wrong, and he feared, rightly so, that the state, with all of its politics, lies, and corruption, would corrupt the church. Williams was not quiet about his opinions, which put him in a dangerous position with the church's leadership. He was finally forced to flee for his life in the dead of winter.

Fortunately for Williams, he had many friends among the native people whose language he spoke. A native village about fifty miles south of Boston took him in and kept him alive over the winter. By spring, Williams began attracting like-minded friends from Massachusetts to come join him in building a new colony in what is now the state of Rhode Island. In time, Williams returned to England and obtained a royal charter to start his new colony based on allowing people of all religions the right to live together without any compulsion to attend this church or that church—or any church for that matter. The colony was a success, and at the time of the American revolution Rhode Island became one of the 13 original states.

About 150 years later, Thomas Jefferson, a framer of the US Constitution, returned to Williams' concept of the importance of separating church and state for the good of each and made this concept a part of the US Constitution. As a result, the United States became the world's first totally secular democracy. In the United States, people are constitutionally free to join the church of their choice—or no church at all if that is what pleases them.

However, as important as religious freedom is, all organized churches are institutions with their own official rules, dogmas, and rituals. Since the Christian Church merged with the Roman Empire in AD 321, the institutional church has become a constant reality. Institutional churches have their own politics and court intrigues, making it difficult to see how these organizations of human beings are capable of furthering the establishment of Jesus's kingdom of God on earth.

We need to recognize that if every human being on earth were to get up tomorrow morning and follow Jesus's teachings, we would be living in a changed world with no more wars, no more killings, no more stealing, no more hatred, no more fear, and no more greed. In truth, if this event were to happen, it could only be described as heaven on earth or the kingdom of God.

Chapter 16

Imagining the Kingdom of God

In conclusion, let us remember Beatle John Lennon's hauntingly beautiful song "Imagine." In his song, John created a list of all the characteristics that his ideal world would contain.

"Imagine" represents a clearly emotional statement that is very close to what Jesus was aiming for with his kingdom of God. Let us pick up where John left off and build on trying to imagine what characteristics Jesus's kingdom of God on earth would have in our time:

1. Imagine no wars. They are only for killing.

2. Imagine no armies. All they do is kill and destroy.

3. Imagine no police. With love in their hearts, people won't need to be policed.

4. Imagine no courts. Where love abounds, there will be no crime and no need for courts.

5. Imagine no lawyers. Where there are no courts, there will be no need for lawyers.

6. Imagine no insurance companies. The kingdom itself will find a way to cover all losses.

7. Imagine no money. It is just a symbol of greed. The people of the kingdom will take care of one another's needs.

8. Imagine no banks. Without money, there is no need for banks.

9. Imagine no companies. Companies just lead to greed, pride, and power, which have no place in the kingdom of God.

10. Imagine there is no government. If there is no money and no crime, there is no need for a government to pass laws about spending money and deciding what actions must be taken to punish criminals.

11. Must have a virtue-advancement plan.

12. Must have a nutrition-distribution plan.

13. Must have a medical plan.

14. Must have doctors, nurses, and medical researchers.

15. Must have an education plan.

16. Must have schools and universities.

17. Must have teachers and professors.

18. Must have a basic scientific research plan.

19. Must have automation and software development for creating the objects and instructions needed to fulfill the people's material needs.

20. Must have an environmental plan.

21. Must have scientists and engineers to fulfill all of the above plans.

22. Must have a wonder club.

23. Must have a humility club.

24. Must have a history club.

25. Must have art, poetry, acting, dance, and music clubs.

26. Must have a Holy Scripture club.

27. Must have a mating club.

28. Must have a celebration club.

29. Must have a ceremonies club.

30. By lottery, everyone will do their share for cleanliness.

31. By lottery, everyone will do their share for construction.

32. By lottery, everyone will do their share for child and adult day care.

33. By lottery, everyone will do their share for sweeping streets, collecting trash and garbage, and providing for sanitation.

34. By lottery, everyone will do their share for end-of-life farewells.

SUMMATION

Jesus and God the Father are one. All Gospel accounts agree that Jesus came not to judge us but to save us. However, Jesus tells us later that the Father has given him the authority to judge, but he doesn't intend to use it on earth. Jesus describes himself as a physician, who has come to cure the sick, but not the well, who do not need his services. As we read deeper into the four Canonical Gospels, it becomes apparent that what Jesus is really saying is that he has come to save many with emotional illnesses caused by their own selfishness.

Jesus's mission on earth is to establish the kingdom of God, but it is unclear whether the kingdom of God will exist here on earth, off in a future heaven, or simply in the heart of believers everywhere. All of these possibilities are suggested in the Gospels, but no hard-and-fast rules are established. Perhaps they are all true.

The people of the kingdom are very different from the people of the world. The people of the world care only about themselves and their own selfish pleasures, but the people of the kingdom care first and foremost about others. Those of the world may steal, covet, or even kill to get what they want. The people of the kingdom are different from the people of the world because of what is in their hearts. The people of the world have hearts filled with lies, fears, hatred, lust, greed, and darkness. The people of the kingdom have hearts full of love, light, humility, faith, compassion, caring, wonder, courage, empathy, benevolence, and affection. What makes the difference? Why do the people of the world live lives of darkness while the people of the kingdom lead lives of light, love, trust, and truth? They are all human beings; why are they so different one from another?

The difference is based on each one's emotional choices. Jesus's main concern is for what is in people's hearts. He has very little concern with their actions, although their actions are often the results of what is in their hearts. The religious authorities of his day are very critical of Jesus's fast-and-loose attitude toward Mosaic law. For Jesus, the Law truly means nothing if there is no virtue within the people's hearts and no good in their actions. Jesus rarely mentions sin—except to say that some notorious sinners are closer to entering the kingdom than are the self-righteous religious authorities—with their heads held high but their hearts full of cruelty and hatred—while the sinners have hearts filled to overflowing with regret, sadness, and anguish.

Jesus calls a band of disciples to assist him in the founding of the kingdom of God. Much later, the disciples will spread the Gospels to all the world. Jesus and his band of disciples move around constantly: healing the sick, exorcising the possessed, and working miracles. He meets many women in his travels. Some of the women seem to instinctively understand who he really is, and they love him dearly because of it. He heals many of these women of both illness and possession. Several of the healed women join his band as caretakers for both Jesus and the disciples. If we were to see his band today, we would think of them as wandering homeless people, which of course, they were.

Two thousand years ago, Jesus and his disciples lived in a pastoral land of grapes and grain and cows and sheep. Jesus often spoke to people in parables that used the language of farming and agriculture to express spiritual principles. Today's scientific and technological society would be unrecognizable for the people of Jesus's time. How can people of our day relate to the Gospel stories from Jesus's time, which are set in a language of cows and grapes and sheep and wheat? In other words, how can we translate cows and grapes into bits and bauds?

This is not an easy question to answer. It is clear that a direct or mindless translation is a useless exercise. Perhaps searching for concepts that offer cross-cultural understanding might be useful. For instance, we already know that emotional memory and responses are very important topics for Jesus. Perhaps we might make progress if we could retell the story about what emotions are kept in someone's heart.

About half of this book is a commentary on how we, living in a scientific age two thousand years later, can view and understand the emotional content of Jesus's words within the four Gospels. Within the commentary, each occurrence of an emotion within Jesus's words is noted, discussed, and explained in ways consistent with our twenty-first-century scientific thinking and ideas.

To do this, I make use of a concept called *duality*, which I am certain was not in existence two thousand years ago. To proceed, we make the following associations. The concept of duality was adopted by Albert Einstein in his 1905 solution to the enigma of the photoelectric effect experiment. Einstein knew that

Newton's particle understanding of light had recently been replaced by Maxwell's wave understanding of light. With the courage of slashing the Gordian knot with a sword, Einstein proposed that a full understanding of the properties of light could only be achieved by creating a concept of wave-particle duality. In Einstein's understanding, light can be thought of as being composed of particles called photons, which Newton had done two hundred years earlier, and at the same time as waves, which Maxwell had recently shown. To fully understand light, it is required to think of light as being simultaneously both a particle and a wave! After Einstein's wave-particle duality, physics was never the same. New doors of conceptual understanding had been opened and would never close again.

Within twenty years, Einstein's light duality had been expanded into a wave-particle duality, which serves as the cornerstone of a new field of physics called quantum mechanics. The wave-particle duality is really just a generalization of Einstein's original concept with added mathematical content to make the concept more general. Quantum mechanics with its wave-particle duality has given physics the conceptual tools to understand the realm of the subatomic world. The success of quantum mechanics has led to atomic energy, modern electronics, communications, and computers. The wave-particle duality has changed our world into something that would not be understandable by people two hundred years ago.

How can the concept of duality be used to understand and talk about human emotions? Let us first point out that the duality concept itself was used by the early Christian Church to explain Jesus's nature. In 385 CE, a church conference in Constantinople agreed that the only way to understand Jesus's nature was as fully human in every way and at the same time fully God! In other words, Jesus himself is a God-human duality!

We now turn to expressing emotion as a duality. Our evolutionary antecedents were a rough bunch. Over the hundreds of thousands of years of human evolution, in our ancestors' fight-or-flight world, the fittest survived for a while, and the weak were eaten right away. Our ancestors came up out of Africa in repeated migrations that eventually filled the world with our kind. Along the way, our ancestors discovered essential facts about living: Hunting-gathering is risky. Farming is hard work. It is easier to steal from farmers than to farm yourself. It is even easier to enslave the farmers, forcing someone else to do the work of feeding you and your kin!

This pattern of enslaving farmers was especially true of tribal people from the Caucus Mountains in what is now central Russia. For example, these particularly warlike people were bad farmers, but they were good robbers and warriors. They spread to the east across what is now Iran, Afghanistan, and India, and into the west through what is now most of Europe. Today, we call them Caucasians (or Aryans), and their descendants live all the way from the west coast of Ireland to southern India.

In order for this succession of war and conquest to continue successfully, the warriors had to become strong and uncaring about the conditions of the people they enslaved. There was a "temptation" within these people to only care about number one!

There is a comic strip character called Hagar the Horrible. Hagar is a not-very-successful Viking chief who takes his little band around Western Europe killing and stealing from other people. When Hagar is at home resting up from all the raping and pillaging of his job, he sits down in his easy chair and reads the Viking news. Above Hagar's head is a sign that reads: "I got mine." Temptation assures us that as long as we follow our own selfish inclinations, we will, in the words of Hagar the Horrible: "Get mine." In order to "get mine" you must first indulge in hate, fear, lying, anger, violence, murder, lust, and greed. The list goes on and on through all of our selfish emotions.

These selfish emotions were never a part of God's plan for us, but God has had to put up with our selfishness because it is needed to drive forward the evolutionary process. God has given us the gift of free will, which makes us free to choose between God's way and our own selfish ways.

What is God's way for us? God's way is called virtue, and in every case, virtue is the antithesis of our own selfishness. For instance, hate is countered by love, fear by courage, lying by truth, and greed by generosity. The list goes on, and like the two sides of an emotional coin, it forms an emotional duality. There are—first, last, and always—a selfish component and a component of God-given virtue in all of our emotions. The duality is bound together by human understanding. There is no sense of courage without fear, no sense of truth without lying, no sense of generosity without greed, and no sense of love without hate. Again, the list goes on.

Jesus, being God, had the ability to sense what emotions were in the hearts of the people he met. In many cases, Jesus was shocked to find that the emotions in some people's hearts were clearly selfish while they were pretending to be kind and upright pillars of the community. This was especially true of religious authorities who wore the fancy clothes of their office, expecting to be treated with respect by all the people they met in the marketplace. Inside their hearts, there was nothing but greed and cunning. Jesus described these people as being like "white tombs, shiny and clean on the outside, but filled with rot and decay on the inside."

What concerned Jesus the most was what he perceived to be within people's hearts. For some people, the situation was reversed. Well-known sinners, like tax collectors and prostitutes, were despised by their communities, but Jesus perceived their hearts to be filled with sadness, remorse, and regret. When a religious authority was boasting that he was glad not to one of "those people" Jesus said that the tax collectors and the prostitutes would enter the kingdom of God long before he would.

Jesus clearly cared far more about what is in people's hearts than to what degree they followed the letter of Mosaic law. Jesus talked very little about sin and a lot about the emotions within a person's heart, and how they could lead a person to commit acts of kindness and goodness. Jesus called this "being fruitful."

Jesus refrains from judgment, but he tells us that the Father has granted to him the power of judgment, which he does not intend to use on earth. Jesus declares that he intends to save us—as a physician would save a dying patient—by healing the problems with our emotional health. The healing process happens right down there in each of our hearts.

Jesus pleads with us to let him turn our emotional coins over from selfishness to God's virtue. The turning of the emotional coins within our hearts is an act of grace on God's part. It is not deserved by us in any way, but it is made possible by God when he hears our true desire for change. It is very important that we ask God to grant our desire to change from selfishness into virtue. We best present our request to God in the form of prayers and meditations. In my own experience, the process of change can be long and slow, but it is worth taking the time to accomplish what must be the highest priority in our lives.

Finally, it is my hope that this book will enable a clear understanding and comprehension of Jesus's teachings for people living in our scientific and technological age. Building the kingdom of God was not just a project for people living two thousand years ago; the project goes on in our day and will continue into the unforeseeable future. We all have a part to do and role to be shared.

Alameda, California
July 1, 2020

allensweet@aasweetphd.com

Printed in the United States
By Bookmasters